RAUSCHENBERG

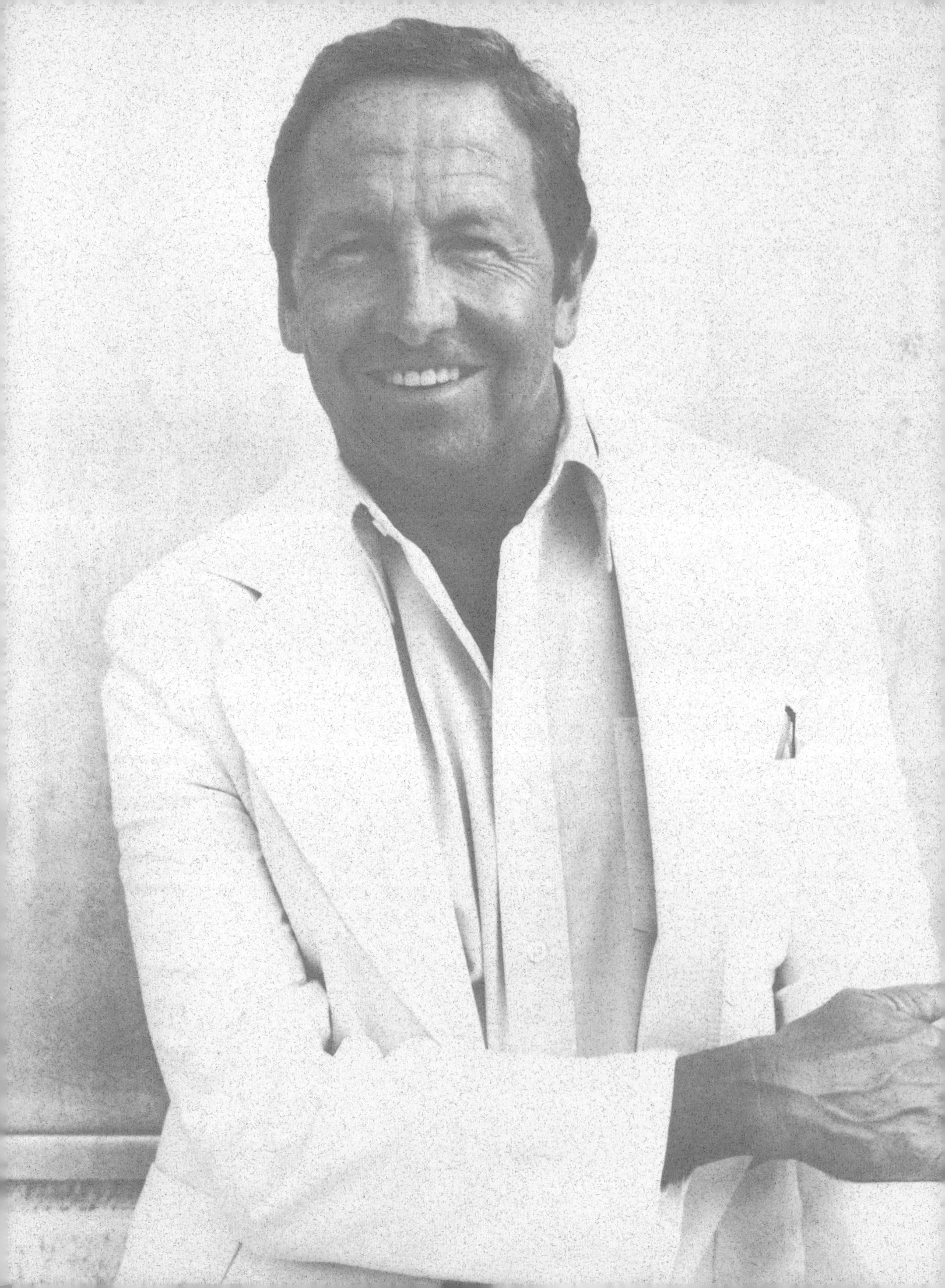

Robert

RAUSCHENBERG

Work

from

Four

Series:

A Sesquicentennial Exhibition

Appreciation by Donald Barthelme

Essay by Linda L. Cathcart

Contemporary Arts Museum

Houston, Texas

This publication has been prepared in conjunction with the exhibition *Robert Rauschenberg, Work from Four Series: A Sesquicentennial Exhibition* organized by Linda L. Cathcart and Marti Mayo for the Contemporary Arts Museum, Houston, and a subsequent state tour.

Contemporary Arts Museum, Houston
December 21, 1985–March 16, 1986

Marion Koogler McNay Art Museum, San Antonio
April 13–June 8, 1986

Dallas Museum of Art, Dallas
December 21, 1986–February 8, 1987

Art Museum of South Texas, Corpus Christi
March 11–June 5, 1987

Robert Rauschenberg, Work from Four Series: A Sesquicentennial Exhibition has been funded in part with grants from the National Endowment for the Arts and the Texas Commission on the Arts with additional support from The Charles Engelhard Foundation, Mr. and Mrs. Fayez Sarofim and Conoco, a Du Pont company.

The Houston presentation has been made possible by the following special friends: Mr. and Mrs. A.L. Ballard, Carolyn Farb, Mr. and Mrs. Jerry E. Finger, Mr. and Mrs. Henry R. Hamman, Mr. and Mrs. I.H. Kempner III, Mr. and Mrs. T.N. Law, Mr. and Mrs. Stewart Orton, Helen Runnells, William F. Stern and Mr. and Mrs. Jimmy J. Younger.

The catalogue is funded through the **Contemporary Arts Publication Fund,** established with the generous support of The Charles Engelhard Foundation in May 1982, with additional support in 1985–1986 from Tenneco Inc.

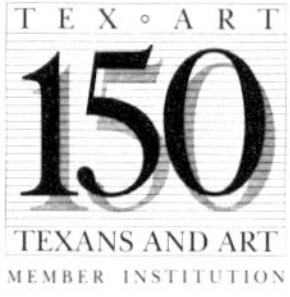

This exhibition is a project of TexArt/150, an association of art museums in Texas committed to celebrating the sesquicentennial anniversary through exhibitions and special programs. TexArt/150 projects are made possible, in part, by grants from Frito-Lay, Inc., the Atlantic Richfield Foundation and Texas Monthly Magazine.

Library of Congress Catalog Card Number 85-72529
ISBN 0-936080-15-9

Table of Contents

Roger I. Davidson, Toronto, Canada

Emil Fray

Sydney Goldfarb

Robert and Jane Meyerhoff, Phoenix, Maryland

Robert Rauschenberg

Terry Van Brunt

Early in 1983, our staff had the idea that Houston's museums should celebrate 1986, the Texas Sesquicentennial year, by presenting major exhibitions of Texas art and artists. This idea was expanded to include museums statewide, and a nonprofit organization, TexArt/150, was formed to enable member institutions to share resources and exhibitions and coordinate fund-raising. TexArt/150 is the first such cooperative effort among the state's art institutions, and we feel that its activities have been successful and precedent-setting.

Robert Rauschenberg, Work from Four Series: A Sesquicentennial Exhibition is the first of three exhibitions of the work of Texas artists being organized by the Contemporary Arts Museum for 1986. Rauschenberg, who was born in Port Arthur, has returned frequently to his native state to visit, to exhibit and to renew the Texan energy and imagery which often have been a part of his work.

The possibility of organizing this exhibition was proposed to Rauschenberg in May 1983 when he was in Houston for an exhibition at the Contemporary Arts Museum documenting his work in dance and theater. It seems appropriate to acknowledge Texas' 150th birthday by celebrating the state's most famous visual artist, an artist whose work embodies an expansiveness which is undeniably Texan in spirit. We are delighted that Rauschenberg agreed to our proposal in spite of a self-imposed hiatus from participating in new projects, called for by his five-year commitment to the Rauschenberg Overseas Culture Interchange (R.O.C.I.), an exhibition which will travel to more than twenty-two countries worldwide.

At the artist's suggestion, we began to plan the exhibition around a body of wall- and floor-dependent works begun in 1981, the "Kabal American Zephyr" series. This series, which until now has been shown only in New York, is a summation and synthesis of many of the artist's concerns and will represent Rauschenberg well to Texas audiences. The artist suggested, and we agreed, that we could place the "Kabal American Zephyrs" in a larger context by including another series which has been seldom exhibited, the "Cardboards" of 1971. As the concept of the exhibition continued to develop, we saw relationships between the "Zephyrs" and "Cardboards" and two additional series, the "Hoarfrosts" and the "Bifocals." All four series have been completed since Rauschenberg made the Captiva, Florida, studio his principal workplace in 1971. They share common materials, such as cardboard, fabrics and solvent-transfer images. They exhibit a common structure, iconography, and composition. They represent the artist at the height of his mature career and exemplify his contribution to the art of our time. We are pleased to present *Robert Rauschenberg, Work from Four Series: A Sesquicentennial Exhibition* to Texas in celebration of its 150th anniversary.

We are grateful for the enthusiastic support of the many people who have assisted with the exhibition and its catalogue. We would first like to thank Bob Rauschenberg, for agreeing to the show, even in the midst of organizing the R.O.C.I. world tour. Special thanks are due to the lenders for their generosity and their willingness to part with works of art for the duration of the exhibition. We would like to thank Donald Barthelme for taking the time from a demanding schedule to contribute insightful and incisive remarks to this catalogue. We asked Mr. Barthelme, a Texan himself, to write an appreciation because of his keen admiration for the artist and because he is a writer who has gained a national reputation while retaining an understanding of the state and its influence on artists.

David White, curator to Robert Rauschenberg, has helped with all aspects of organizing the exhibition and preparing the catalogue. He has taken time to share both his records and his knowledge of the artist's work and career for the documentation and chronology, and has given us information and advice at every stage. Nicholas Howie, assistant to Robert Rauschenberg in New York, has rendered valuable aid at several points in this effort. Bradley Fray, Rauschenberg's assistant in Captiva, answered our questions by facilitating communication between us and the artist and organizing a free flow of information among all parties. Donald Saff and Brenda Woodard of the R.O.C.I. staff have helped with scheduling. Terry Van Brunt, who works with the artist, provided the video which accompanies the show and coordinated many other important aspects of the project. We owe general thanks to all members of Rauschenberg's staff, both in Florida and New York. They have been unfailingly courteous and helpful.

Leo Castelli Gallery and Sonnabend Gallery cooperated with us in all our requests. The Museum of Fine Arts, Houston library made available their resources for our research, and many museums and galleries around the world supplied information in response to our innumerable queries. Karen Lee Spaulding and Polly Morrice edited the catalogue with attention and skill.

The entire staff of the Contemporary Arts Museum contributed to the smooth and successful organization of this endeavor. Nina Nathan Schroeder and Carolyn Vaughan prepared the exhibition histories and bibliography, and Carolyn Vaughan assisted with all aspects of the exhibition and catalogue. Cheryl Blissitte, secretary to the director; Lou Cinda Holt and Cece Goodell of the registrar's office; Michael Barry, head preparator; and Sally Johnson, public information officer, provided special assistance.

We would also like to express appreciation to the directors and staffs of other Texas museums hosting the exhibition for sharing our enthusiasm for the project: John Palmer Leeper of the Marion Koogler McNay Art Museum, San Antonio; Harry S. Parker III of the Dallas Museum of Art; and Ric Collier of the Art Museum of South Texas, Corpus Christi.

Through the efforts of Pamela A. Riddle, the Contemporary Arts Museum's development officer, and her staff, financial support for the exhibition has been provided by grants from the National Endowment for the Arts, the Texas Commission on the Arts and TexArt/150, with additional support from The Charles Engelhard Foundation, Mr. and Mrs. Fayez Sarofim and Conoco, a Du Pont company. The publication of the catalogue has been made possible through the *Contemporary Arts Publication Fund*, established with the generous support of The Charles Engelhard Foundation in May 1982, with additional support in 1985–1986 from Tenneco Inc. The Houston presentation of the exhibition has been funded by a group of special friends of the Museum. We are most grateful to all of these sponsors for their commitment to this important and exciting project.

Linda L. Cathcart
Director

Marti Mayo
Curator

Being Bad

by Donald Barthelme

Rauschenberg's problem (one of Rauschenberg's problems) is how to be bad for thirty years or more. To sustain a high level of misbehavior over a third of a century is not the easiest of tasks. The German writer Heimeto von Doderer put it this way: "One begins by breaking windows. Then one becomes a window oneself."

Rauschenberg has tried as hard as anyone to be nonacceptable but early (and rather cheerfully) discovered that nothing is nonacceptable. Consider the variety and ingenuity of recent efforts in this direction. X whittles upon his penis, Y jumps out of windows, and Z, that dirty dog, paints East Hampton domestic interiors. MTV has severely compromised surrealism, perhaps ruined it forever, and Michael Graves is giving wretched excess a bad name. Beuys is in trouble; what's a boy to do when his fat melts? David Salle and Eric Fischl are looking more and more lamblike every day. And so on.

The difficulty here is not producing mere run-of-the-mill outrageousness, but the nature of the transformational process by which aspects of the world are made over into art. How to prevent the ugly (what we have agreed to call ugly) from becoming, in some sense, beautiful (what we now agree to call beautiful) over time, thus losing the electrical charge which made the artist choose it in the first place? You can't. But there are strategies of delay. Céline, with the aid of some truly revolting politics, managed to remain a monster almost to the end.

The transfiguration of the commonplace, in Arthur Danto's phrase, is both Rauschenberg's fundamental maneuver and his dilemma. He is particularly adept with that wonderful category, the messy, having studied same, no doubt, with de Kooning, who managed to be messier than Hans Hofmann, who now appears positively tidy. In 1962, visiting Rauschenberg's studio with the photographer Rudy Burkhardt, I noticed that the windows overlooking Broadway were dark gray with our good New York grime. Rauschenberg was then working on some of the earliest of his black-and-white silkscreen paintings, and the tonality of the paintings was very much that of the windows. We ran a shot of the windows alongside photographs of the paintings in the journal I was then laboring for—instant art history. New York is a great filthy gift, and its very filthiness has worked to the artist's advantage, has been tonic. Robert Hughes observes (quoting highly placed officials at the New York City dump) that Manhattan throws away more manufactured goods in a week than eighteenth-century France produced in a year, and the artist's use of these portable stigmata has been richly proportionate.

The photomechanical silkscreen, too, expands the bin of materials available to the collagist enormously. It provides access to anything that has ever been photographed, allows quotation at great length and at any scale. It permits superimposition of one image upon another in such a way that the first bleeds through the second, as physical collage does not—that is, it allows a heightened degree of messiness. The colors of the original image can be changed as the artist wishes. Parody is possible, even color-scandal à la Warhol. The process adapts to almost any surface; you can silkscreen onto veils or eggs or the mayor. No other artist has found so many brilliant uses for it, and in no other hands has its combination with orphaned objects been so potent.

There are constants within this welter of possibilities. Take for example his use of the familiar brown corrugated cardboard shipping carton, which presents itself again and again in his work. Flattened and torn, it invariably yields strong shapes (a fact not unknown to Schwitters). As *a thing* it is the very definition of mundanity, trash from birth—perhaps only the gray, hopeless shirt cardboard has less social status. To insist upon it is, metaphorically, to condemn the system of value in which its status is seen as abysmal. To say that other people have used the same or similar objects for the purposes of art or that the object is presented not ponderously but often with a deliberate gaiety misses the point, which is that the artist has chosen it repeatedly, that he is in some way committed to it. Rauschenberg will almost always pick the rough over the smooth, the flawed over the whole, the old over the new, but so, too, will many other artists. A procedure based on such choices requires that the ensemble be *bad enough*—that is, distinct enough from all other sights to allow itself to be seen, to take hold, even to prevail in a visual landscape that is already clamorous. Windows again: "The works had to look at least as interesting as anything that was going on outside the window," Rauschenberg says.

The artist seeks a construction that holds the viewer in a certain sort of tension, and it is in being able to pull this off, year after year, that major reputations are made and endure. One's own achievements become what must be circumvented. Rauschenberg excels, as he must, in getting to the left of his own history. He manages this by what can only be called acts of poetic intuition. If the basic principle of collage is the juxtaposition of unlike things within a visual field (in Rauschenberg's case, most often what Leo Steinberg has aptly termed the "work surface picture plane"), he need in theory only find stranger and stranger things and build not-quite-decipherable rebuses from them. The theory is straightforward enough but, of course, inadequate. It ignores the true source of this artist's power, which lies in the mystery of particular choices. Charles Mauron, writing of the reception of the early work of Mallarmé, notes that although readers felt rebuffed, excluded by the work, they nevertheless also knew it to be magnificently written. Seizure, as it were, is always prior to understanding. It is an essential aspect of the tension mentioned earlier, and it is where Rauschenberg's real genius lies—the tire wrestled over the goat's hind legs.

Robert Rauschenberg, Work from Four Series

by Linda L. Cathcart

Robert Rauschenberg's pieces of art are alive— they are so filled with life, in fact, that the uninitiated viewer may be tempted to dismiss them as not being art. Rauschenberg belongs to a generation of artists who share his concern that vitality alone be enough to ensure art; among his fellows are artists Jasper Johns, Roy Lichtenstein, Claes Oldenburg, James Rosenquist, Andy Warhol, and dancers and musicians Trisha Brown, John Cage and Merce Cunningham.

Like his contemporaries whose inspiration comes from the everyday, Rauschenberg finds that vital art requires the participation of both artist and audience. He believes greatly in the power of art and art-making to go hand in hand with life, to be a necessary, sustaining force.

Rauschenberg's success as an artist continues despite an often-heard voice that says one type of artistic expression is made obsolete by the next. Rauschenberg's art remains his own—while acknowledging his respect for the traditions of abstract painting and of collage— and in turn it is admired and reflected upon by the generation of artists now coming of age.

If there is one constant in Robert Rauschenberg's work, it is that the pictures are as difficult to comprehend now as when he first began working. One may prefer the older paintings because one is used to them, but because Rauschenberg's art is made from (his) life, it has always been unpredictable and diverse. Its next move is difficult to anticipate, thus confusing some—those who wish art to be constantly self-refining and always following the path of its original inspiration.

The imagery Rauschenberg uses is always "found"—he never creates it himself. This engenders a specific kind of excitement. As his audience, we are left both to speculate about his imagery and to participate in its completeness. If the work were definably figurative and narrative, our task would be made easier, but it is not. Rauschenberg does not paint his portrait, a lucky cat, a bomber, into the canvas. These things find their way there through the vitality which makes the pictures. They come from life. Rauschenberg believes in abstraction—one made from life, not from theory. He combines technique and form to create vitality and this makes his art different from conventional modern painting.

In order to compose his pictures, Rauschenberg seemingly uses two methods—he selects a few images and waits for the rest of the picture to suggest itself or he decides on an overall look and begins to fill in the picture, apparently regardless of considerations of scale and composition. The parts themselves do not matter so much as does the friction between them which gives credibility to the pictures.

By recognizing the pictorial possibilities of both images and objects, as well as the spaces between them, Rauschenberg makes art which is seemingly whole and direct, yet actually difficult to see and to comprehend. There is nothing to walk around in—no place to project yourself as a viewer into these two-dimensional works. Many pictures have attachments. There are doors which do not open, umbrellas flattened on the surfaces of the canvas. Some works are three-dimensional sculptures, but these most often utilize symmetrical objects which can be as easily apprehended from one view as from another. All the work is frontal—even the "Bifocal" series, which are free-hanging paintings. Each side of the paintings forms but an element of the whole, yet we can only apprehend one side at a time. By focusing on the disenfranchised, disassociated, deterred object, Rauschenberg has turned its realism against its materialism. Rather than invent, he observes to produce an abstraction. As a means of establishing a new vocabulary for formal concerns, Rauschenberg uses an unorthodox matching of images. One can see by his use of light—not painted, but created physically from within the structures—that he means the images to exist in multiple layers and to extend beyond the pictures' edges. In this respect, he denies the tradition which says an abstract art must be self-contained and self-referential.

Rauschenberg uses the technique of layering to great advantage in his "Hoarfrost" series. Here, the physical separations he literally sandwiches between fabric and images make the pieces breathe—they float and ripple on the wall, disturbed by the slightest breeze or movement. Some magic inhabits there. The artist has captured the effect of veils of paint, layers of color and translucency, for his own. He uses it for an illusionism which is whole, complete and finally abstract. These veils are effective art because Rauschenberg establishes no barrier between them and the viewer. Yet everything in the pictures distances itself from us. This is the power of Rauschenberg's art: the works are particular, yet the images remain separate and diverse.

What is true of the work from these series is true of all of Rauschenberg's work. In it, he uses the real world not as reality, but as a repository of images and ideas from which he can recreate original visual emotions. Using multiple layers of support material and images, he achieves endless combinations which provide ever new information with personal resonance. What happens inside the frame may be chaotic and the pictures and sculptures may project into our space, but the ultimate aim is not to fill conventional pictorial space. It is to create illusion—not replicate reality.

Rauschenberg uses a combination of techniques—silkscreen, freehand painting, collage and assemblage. His ability is to grasp the visual possibilities of techniques and materials, and combine them in an art which is as complex or as simple as he chooses. He dances with every partner—he asks for the time and distorts it, he adopts photography and then defaces it, he admires the masters and teases them.

Rauschenberg's art sometimes seems almost disconcertingly normal. The images are all things we know. The "Cardboards," for example, are made of unadorned cardboard boxes. Shaped and flattened by the artist, these boxes—objects discarded everywhere—are composed into artworks. They are awkward, almost inarticulate, and are Rauschenberg's way of showing he can take or leave technology. Having completed many sophisticated projects using high technology, Rauschenberg demonstrates that the cardboard container can be just as satisfactory to him.

Rauschenberg's love of physically displacing the viewer in relation to his work reaches its most extreme possibility in the "Kabal American Zephyr" series. Made up of highly disparate parts joined in unusual and often very erotic ways, these objects share with traditional sculpture the rhythmic collision of their parts to create a balance of positive and negative space. Unlike typical sculpture, however, these works do not depend upon a harmony of juxtaposed pleasing shapes. Instead, Rauschenberg crashes into the gallery with great lumps of material—some precious, some gross—combined with a particular attitude which reveals careful study of street life in cities from Port Arthur, Texas, to New York City. There is nothing subtle about these sculptures. Rauschenberg juxtaposes images and objects of great beauty, such as a length of almost transparent silk, with those of great hideousness, like a shred of old tire; he sets things on a huge scale—a giant American flag—against tiny pieces: a bit of Chinese calligraphy. The whole experience of the work is one of unexpectedness, yet it suggests with great accuracy the emotional quality of our world.

In his recent works, Rauschenberg questions the modern artistic premise that each area in an artwork must be of equal importance to every other and have been given "quality" attention by the artist. This is not the way we perceive the real world. Once Rauschenberg adopted this principle, he opened his art to all kinds of new possibilities. Rauschenberg can see one part of his work in great detail and another part of the same canvas in utter generality. He can make a picture of many parts and into each part he can put as many or as few things as he likes; yet he is still able to unite the whole. It is a moment of reconciled factions, in which every competing part retains its essential characteristics.

Rauschenberg's ability to penetrate reality to produce abstraction—to use the materialism of reality against reality—makes him one of the great modern artists. From him, later abstractionists whose images came from "real life" learned how to invent from observation, rather than to replicate or narrate. Because Rauschenberg's art is taken from life, it is full of events as well as emptiness. The images in his paintings strike us as unbalanced and the objects in the sculpture, strangely joined. He seems to be striving for no one object, color or emotion to dominate—however, as in real life, certain objects are loaded with meaning and draw the viewer's eye. Each piece is like a conversation, complete with awkward pauses, silences and stammers, as well as graceful phrases. The effect is marvelous and gives far greater coherence to the work than can be found in invented compositions. Because Rauschenberg's art is breathing and alive, it resists our efforts to organize its moments. This resistance is its most arresting quality. Each area is indivisible from every other on the surface, and even the surface of a work is often indivisible from the rhythm of life around it.

To see that Robert Rauschenberg pursues all aspects of life one has only to read the chronology included in this catalogue. He embraces causes, establishes foundations, encourages other artists. His social commitments bring a quality of shared experience and common emotion to his art. Rauschenberg's art is endearingly human—it flaps from supports, it jumps out into the room, it dangles, drags, rots and sags. It has no pretensions to control except as art. It is flat but not contained; it is pictorial, but not coherent. Above all, Rauschenberg's art convinces the viewer it is worthwhile to stop and sort out all the parts.

Rauschenberg continues to make an art which, if we are to understand it fully, requires us to indulge both it

and ourselves. He manages to combine the mechanical
and the natural, and still create works which are, with-
out being naive, almost childlike in their purity. To
participate, we must give up longing for traditional
unity, and respond freely and indulgently. To share in
Rauschenberg's art, we must grasp the crude and igno-
rant parts of his pieces, as well as the beautiful and
ethereal ones, and admire his art for what it is. From
art's point of view, it is an art which continues to build
the road laid down by Kurt Schwitters and Marcel
Duchamp. From life's point of view, Rauschenberg's
is an art which selects from the street, the skyline, the
crowds, from the humblest objects; an art which reso-
nates in memory and pushes at our conscious intel-
lectual knowledge of his predecessors' great pictures.

In modern art, the gestures of brush stroke, the size
of support, the choice of materials have come to defy
our abilities to apprehend them—they are too large,
too fast, too strange. This makes us long for objects
contained and discrete and finally knowable. Robert
Rauschenberg's recent art continues to put off this
desire in order to extend itself. He draws on the
American tradition of abstraction using images from
immediate sources; this he combines with the knowledge that good abstraction can expand, rather than
encapsulate, our visual vocabulary. Abstraction, he
has found out, need not be rigid or rulebound, or even
exclude representation. For Robert Rauschenberg,
there is no limit in size, scale, content, imagery or
comparison with the real world necessary to make
his art. Nor should there be any limits to our
enjoyment of it.

Chronology

compiled by Marti Mayo

This chronology covers the years 1976 to 1986, with the exception of events related directly to works made before 1976 included in the exhibition. No information is included here on limited edition prints, books or other multiples, and the only exhibitions mentioned are those in which works from series in this catalogue were first shown. An exhibition history and bibliography can be found on page 66. For information on the years prior to 1976, refer to Robert Rauschenberg, Washington, D.C.: National Collection of Fine Arts, Smithsonian Institution, 1976.

Unattributed quotations are from an interview between the artist and Marti Mayo in Washington, D.C., October 31, 1985.

1971

Establishes permanent residence and studio on Captiva Island, Florida. Captiva becomes his principal workplace; he continues to maintain New York house.

Begins "Cardboard" series, which will be the first body of work completed in the new studio. The "Cardboards" are first exhibited at Leo Castelli Gallery, New York.

"I was too sensitive to do driftwood and shell sculptures; everything was the same kind of beachcraft. I was trying to wean myself from urban imagery. I was in a different environment. Cardboard boxes are everywhere."

As in the past, during the years 1971 to 1986 Rauschenberg makes works with common elements, which he groups into series. However he also creates numerous works which are not identified as part of any series.

With Robert Petersen, establishes Untitled Press, Inc., a lithographic studio in Captiva.

1972

Establishes close working relationship with Graphicstudio, University of South Florida, Tampa, directed by Donald Saff. Saff later becomes artistic director of the Rauschenberg Overseas Culture Interchange (R.O.C.I.) project.

1974

Begins "Hoarfrost" series. Works from the series first shown in December at Leo Castelli Gallery and Sonnabend Gallery, New York.

1976

Continues work on "Jammer" series begun in 1975. The "Jammers" are simple compositions of fabric and poles. Devoid of any imagery, they suggest nautical associations both in the titles of each piece and in their forms, which are reminiscent of sails.

First retrospective exhibition since 1965 opens at National Collection of Fine Arts, Smithsonian Institution, Washington, D.C., and travels throughout the United States. The artist assists with each of the five installations. Repeated exposure to his early work contributes to his general need for new and foreign experiences to satisfy what Rauschenberg terms "a chronic restlessness." Throughout his career he has translated this restlessness from his life into his art.

First living visual artist to be featured on the cover of *Time*, November 29 issue. Image is a collage titled *Rauschenberg by Rauschenberg*. In the accompanying article, "The Most Living Artist," Robert Hughes writes:

"With his anarchic sweetness and prodigal talent, Rauschenberg, now 51, has for the best part of 25 years been the enfant terrible of American modernism: a permanent scalawag, handing out indulgences to all comers. He is a model of the joy of art."

Concentrates on making two series, "Spreads" and "Scales." A few works in these series date from late 1975. These large assemblages combine many techniques, images and objects into rigidly composed, wall-dependent works, baroque encyclopedias of his many interests. In an *Art News* review of the first exhibition of these series at Leo Castelli Gallery and Sonnabend Gallery, New York, the critic William Zimmer writes of the "Spreads" and "Scales":
"In recent years the artist has left everything out, the 'Jammers' being the prime example. Perhaps stimulated by his retrospective…Rauschenberg has put everything in again."

Spends several weeks in Dallas, working on a film with composer David Tudor and the Viola Farber Dance Company. The film, *Brazos River*, documents a dance in which the dancers' movement creates electronic sound. Designs sets which, at appropriate times, function as costumes for the dancers.

Campaigns on Capitol Hill with artist James Rosenquist and arts advocate Rubin Gorewitz for a national bill to reinstate a law which would make artists eligible to receive tax deductions for donating their own works to museums and other nonprofit institutions. Rauschenberg's concern for the rights of artists has been evident throughout his career and his altruism has benefited many colleagues and young artists. He has campaigned for and endorsed many political and artists' rights issues.

Receives Logan Prize, The Art Institute of Chicago.

Receives honorary doctorate in fine arts, University of South Florida, Tampa.

1977

Creates the sets and costumes for *Travelogue*, a dance premiering at the Minskoff Theatre, New York, January 18. The piece is a collaboration with the Merce Cunningham Dance Company and includes music by John Cage. It is a reunion of these three artists, who worked together extensively in the fifties and sixties, and marks their first collaboration in thirteen years. The costumes are colorful and elegant, reminiscent of the works in the "Jammers" series.

Commissioned by the Fort Worth Art Museum to create a work for the permanent collection. *Whistle Stop*, 1978, is typical of the "Spreads." It is dedicated to the artist's father.

Made an honorary citizen of Fort Worth by Mayor Hugh Palmer.

With James Rosenquist, is invited to participate in exhibition *The Florida Connection*, Jacksonville Art Museum, recognizing two important contemporary artists living and working in Florida.

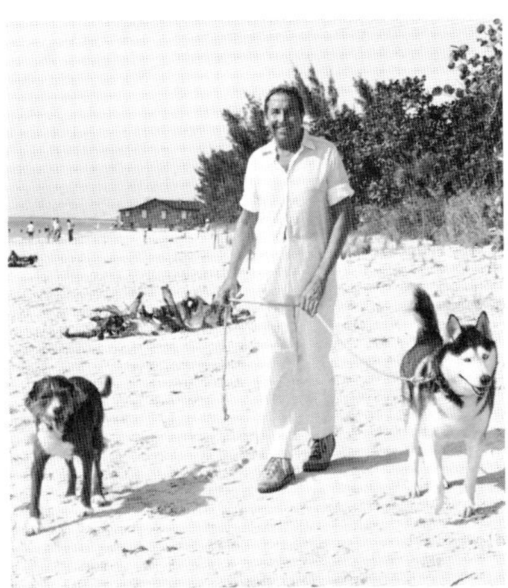

Robert Rauschenberg on Captiva Island with his dogs, 1982

The Merce Cunningham Dance Company performing *Travelogue*, 1977, with set by Robert Rauschenberg

Participates in exhibition, *Five from Louisiana*, New Orleans Museum of Art. Creates *Opal Reunion (Spread)*, 1976, especially for the exhibition.

"That year I was a native son of three states. I told them I was from Texas and they said that was close enough."

Establishes a medical assistance fund through Change, Inc., a nonprofit organization Rauschenberg founded in 1970 to provide emergency funds for artists. Administered by the Hospital for Joint Diseases in New York, the program enables qualified artists to receive medical attention in exchange for works of art donated by collectors to participating hospitals.

Continuing his involvement with artists' rights, participates in June 27 panel discussion on the role of government in supporting the arts. Panel members include Rubin Gorewitz and sculptor Richard Mayer. Discussion is sponsored by the Northern California branch of Artists' Equity, held at University of California Extension Center, San Francisco. It centers on ramifications of California's passage, the previous year, of the Resale and Royalties Act for works of art.

Receives Mayor's Award of Honor in Arts and Culture, Mayor's Commission for Cultural Affairs, New York.

Named to Board of Directors, Institute for Art and Urban Resources, P.S.1, Long Island City, New York.

1978

Continues work on "Spreads" and "Scales."

First shows *Hiccups*, 1978, a 62-foot long drawing composed of 97 units connected by zippers: included in exhibition *Works from Captiva*, Vancouver Art Gallery, Canada. Each unit consists of solvent transfer images with fabric collage on handmade paper.

Begins serving as Chairman, Board of Directors, Trisha Brown Company. Central in the development of contemporary avant-garde dance, Trisha Brown was a member of the Judson Church Dance Theatre and the Grand Union Dance Company in the sixties, before forming the Trisha Brown Company in 1970. Rauschenberg had been associated with the Judson Church group in its formative years and worked with many of its members, including Brown, to create performance and dance works.

Receives Creative Arts Award for painting, Brandeis University, Waltham, Massachusetts.

Elected member of the American Academy of Arts and Sciences, Cambridge, Massachusetts.

1979

Continues work on "Spreads" and "Scales."

Begins work on *Bank Job*, 1979, a 29-foot long commission from the Equitable Trust in Baltimore for its new corporate headquarters. It is first shown in the premiere exhibition at Leo Castelli Gallery/Greene Street, New York, and dedicated at the Equitable Bank Center, May 17, 1981.

Creates *Piece for Tropic* as cover for *The Miami Herald Tropic Magazine*, Sunday, December 30. Image printed in an edition of 600,000, making it largest limited edition artwork in history. One hundred signed copies of the blue, red and black collage of Rauschenberg's own photographs taken in Florida are delivered at random to regular subscribers. Project initiated by the newspaper to honor the artist.

Designs set and costumes for Trisha Brown's *Glacial Decoy*, first performed at Marymount Manhattan College Theater, New York, June 20–24. Marks the first major artistic collaboration between Brown and a visual artist. Rauschenberg's set consists of hundreds of images—photographs taken by the artist in and around Fort Myers, Florida—flashing continuously on a screen behind the dancers. The clicking of the projectors as the images change provides sound for the dance. Costumes are loose, white, pleated, translucent gowns with bell-shaped sleeves.

Included in *Inside New York's Art World*, a book of interviews by Barbaralee Diamondstein. Interviewed with other major figures in contemporary art and architecture, Rauschenberg contributes to the literature on his own work and the artistic milieu of New York in the fifties and sixties.

Wins Grand Prize, International Exhibition of Graphic Art, Ljubljana, Yugoslavia.

Receives Special Award, Eighth Graphic Arts Biennale, Krakow, Poland.

Awarded Gold Medal for Graphics, Oslo.

1980

Continues "Spreads" and "Scales." Begins series called "Cloisters," consisting of solvent transfer images and collage mounted on plywood. Also begins "Signal" series of small, square works similar to the "Spreads" and composed of photographic images transferred to plywood panels.

Commissioned by Rockefeller Center Development Corporation to create *Fargo Podium*, 1981, a three-dimensional mixed-media installation for the new Wells Fargo Building, Los Angeles. *Fargo Podium* is environmental in nature; viewers walk over floor sections and sit on sculptural elements.

Creates *Periwinkle Shaft*, 1979–1980, dedicated on October 3, a commission for the Children's Hospital Medical Center in Washington, D.C. The two-part work, typical of the "Spreads," incorporates mirrors and is installed in an escalator shaft; one part is visible as viewers ascend first escalator, the second appearing as they proceed to the next level. The mirrors reflect both viewers and each part of the work into the other part.

Subject of book, *Off the Wall: Robert Rauschenberg and the Art World of Our Time*, by Calvin Tomkins. Book focuses on Rauschenberg's life and work to describe the tumultuous New York art world of the sixties and early seventies.

Elected foreign member of the Royal Academy of Fine Arts, Stockholm.

1981

Continues "Spreads" and "Scales." Begins work on new series, "Kabal American Zephyr." The series and the titles of the works are inspired by a catalogue, *The Bizarre Imagery of Yoshitoshi: The Herbert R. Cole Collection*, published by the Los Angeles County Museum of Art, 1980. Tsukioka Yoshitoshi (1839–1892) was a

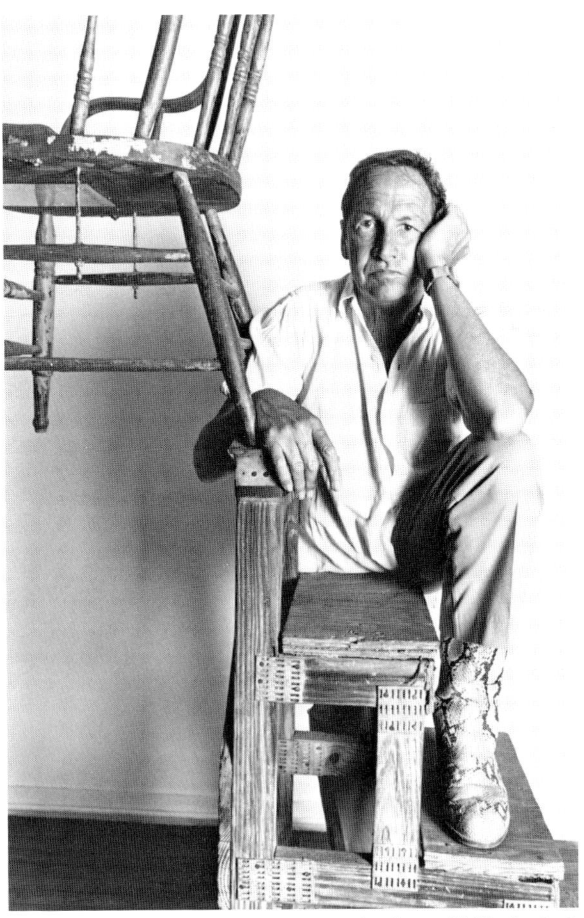

Robert Rauschenberg with *The Ancient Incident (Kabal American Zephyr)*, 1981

Japanese print artist and illustrator of books and newspapers. Famous during his lifetime, his work was largely forgotten after his death. A rediscovery and reevaluation began in the sixties, his brutal imagery and brilliant color proving interesting to contemporary audiences. At first, Rauschenberg selects titles for the "Zephyrs" directly from works by Yoshitoshi, such as *Demons of Illness and Poverty Stalking the Lucky Gods*. Rauschenberg says,
"Later I learned how to do the titles myself. I picked up on his cadences."
Subsequent titles of works in this series—*The Vain Convoy of Europe Out West*, 1982—are composed by Rauschenberg. The inspiration from a foreign culture and another century exemplifies the kind of artistic stimulation he has sought since his 1976 retrospective.

Begins work on *The ¼ Mile or 2 Furlong Piece*, which he intends to be the longest artwork in the world. First section exhibited at Edison Community College, Fort Myers, Florida, February 1982; the second completed section also shown there, July 1983. Both sections are exhibited at the Center for Fine Arts, Miami, May–June 1984. The work can be seen as "a retrospective of a whole life in art," according to James Cain, chairman of the fine arts department, Edison Community College. The finished portion of the work consists of 190 feet of joined panels of different heights hung in order of completion. Still in progress, the work utilizes the techniques Rauschenberg has employed over his career.

Makes "Photems" series, groups of photographs stacked one above the other in a totemlike fashion and mounted on aluminum panels.

Robert Rauschenberg Photographs published by Pantheon Books in conjunction with a major exhibition of photographs at the Centre Georges Pompidou, Paris. The book contains selected images from 1945–1969 and work from 1979–1980. The newer photographs are occasioned by the artist's increased involvement with

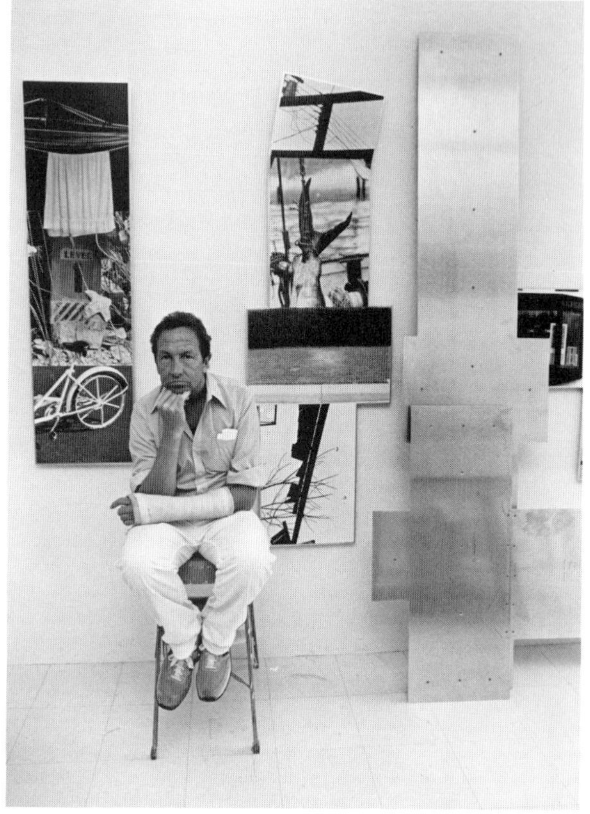

Robert Rauschenberg in his Captiva Studio working on "Photems" in 1981

the camera, sparked by the shooting of enormous numbers of images for Trisha Brown's *Glacial Decoy.* Has continued to photograph here and abroad, and since 1979 has had numerous exhibitions of this work.

Assists in organizing a benefit art auction for Trisha Brown Company, Leo Castelli Gallery/Greene Street, New York, May 16–30. Designs poster.

Featured on CBS TV's "Sunday Morning," February 22, at work in Captiva studio.

Creates design for Hubert Humphrey Human Rights Award.

Named Member, Board of Directors, Association Internationale de Défence des Artistes–U.S.A., an organization which defends the rights of artists of all disciplines who are victims of political oppression in any country.

Made an Officer, Ordre des Arts et Lettres, Ministry of Culture and Communication, France.

Designated Fellow of the Rhode Island School of Design, Providence.

1982

Continues both "Spread" and "Kabal American Zephyr" series.

Begins "Bifocal" series: two-sided works made of fabric collaged to cardboard. The "Bifocals," relating in both imagery and form to the "Zephyr" series, are the artist's further explorations into double-sided works which exist in the nebulous territory between painting and sculpture.

Travels to China, June–July. For a project initiated by Gemini G.E.L., creates 491 collages using Chinese ideograms and local materials such as silk and paper, which is produced to his specifications by China's oldest paper mill. While in China, his idea for the major project *Rauschenberg Overseas Culture Interchange* (R.O.C.I.) coalesces. He has been considering working in foreign cultures using local materials and imagery since 1977, following his retrospective. One of his strongest impressions in China, he says, is the power of art to reach from one person to another across political and cultural divisions. He is excited by the

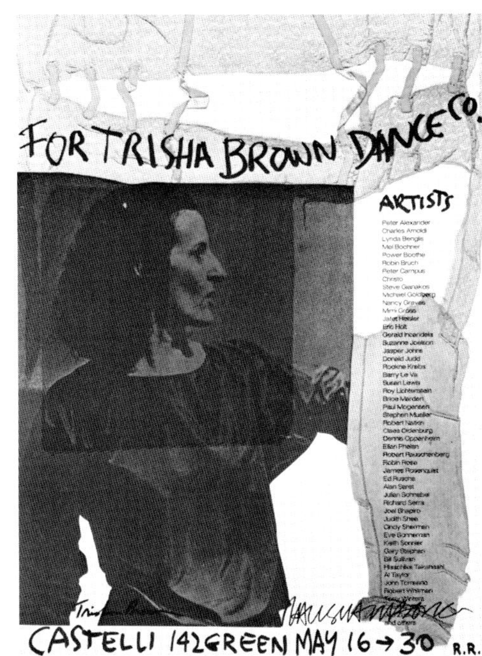

Poster design for
Trisha Brown
Company benefit,
1981

idea that someone who has never been more than a few miles from his isolated village can experience contemporary art.

On leaving China, travels to Japan to produce a body of ceramic works, the series "Japanese Clayworks" and "Japanese Recreational Clayworks," at the Otsuka Otimi Ceramic Company in Shigaraki.

After returning from China and Japan, makes a 100-foot continuous color photographic collage from photographs taken in China. *Chinese Summerhall* is produced at Graphicstudio II, University of South Florida, Tampa.
"It was something for over the mantel, you know."

Receives the Skowhegan Medal for Painting, Skowhegan College, Maine.

1983
Exhibits works from "Kabal American Zephyr" series at Sonnabend Gallery and 112 Greene Street, New York. Concurrently, shows some of the Chinese collages, "Japanese Clayworks" and *Chinese Summerhill*, at Leo Castelli Gallery/Greene Street. Additional Chinese collages exhibited at The Museum of Modern Art. Robert Hughes comments in *Time* magazine:
"There are now by latest count four Rauschenberg shows running in Manhattan…They are all pendants to a larger project, The Rauschenberg Overseas Culture Interchange (R.O.C.I.), whereby he intends to travel and exhibit a changing nucleus of works in some 20 countries while working on new projects with local artists and craftsmen…It is clear from the New York shows that out of this pharaonic enterprise, Rauschenberg has been producing some of the best works of his career."

Designs set and costumes for *Set and Reset*, choreography by Trisha Brown and music by Laurie Anderson, for the Trisha Brown Company. The work is first presented at the Brooklyn Academy of Music's Next Wave Fall Festival, October 20–23. Rauschenberg creates a

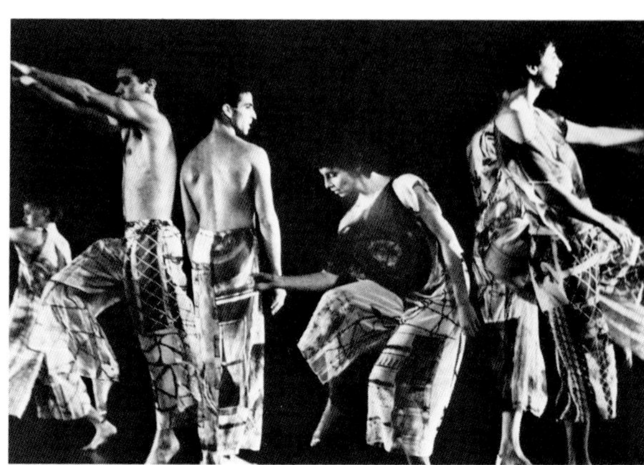

Trisha Brown Company in *Set and Reset*, 1983, with set and costumes designed by Robert Rauschenberg

monumental free-standing sculpture, *Elastic Carrier: Shiner.* Four separate black-and-white film montages are projected onto the translucent fabric surfaces of this 36-by-11 foot geometric structure (two three-dimensional triangles on either side of a cube) producing a complex and shifting layering of images. As the piece begins, the sculpture stands on stage with the sound track of the films running. Gradually, it is raised twelve feet above the floor, as Rauschenberg's sound track is replaced by Anderson's score. The dancers wear translucent costumes silkscreened with black-and-white photographic images of architectural details, recalling filmed sequences appearing on the set.

Travels to Thailand and Sri Lanka and produces works in both countries. This is a planning and research trip, further establishing the viability of the R.O.C.I. tour.

In December, begins work on the "Salvage" series. These paintings consist of silkscreened and collaged images, using his own photographs, inspired by the most recent collaboration with Trisha Brown.

Receives Bronze Award, International Exhibition of Graphic Art, Ljubljana, Yugoslavia.

1984

Continues "Salvage" series.
Working trips to Mexico and Chile in preparation for R.O.C.I. exhibitions in those countries.

Exhibition in hometown, Port Arthur, Texas. In conjunction with the exhibition, creates a print and poster to be used to raise funds for the Robert Rauschenberg Scholarship Fund, Lamar University at Port Arthur, a general fund for students who show academic ability and financial need. Currently, eight students are receiving financial aid.

The Trisha Brown Company performs *Set and Reset* in Houston, May 16–17, sponsored by the Contemporary Arts Museum in conjunction with the Houston presentation of the exhibition *Rauschenberg/Performance.*

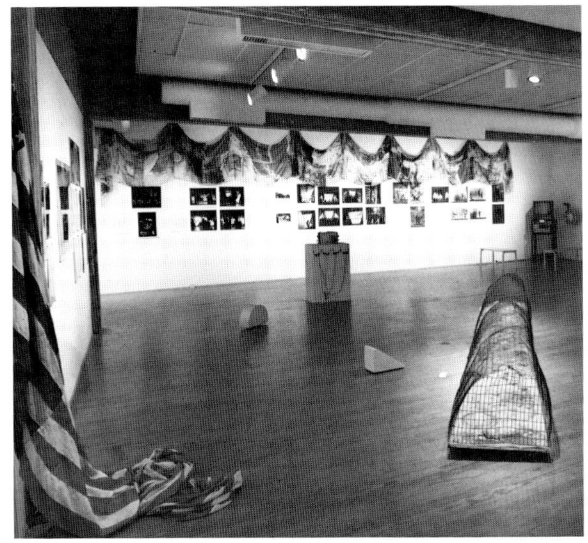

Installation view of *Rauschenberg/ Performance* in Houston, 1984

In August, attends launch of space shuttle Discovery during which he is photographed by *Life* magazine with a work-in-progress. *Life* reports,
"One of 70 artists chosen by N.A.S.A. to portray the shuttle, Robert Rauschenberg, 58, wants a free ride as a truly aesthetic experience."

Announces scope and intention of R.O.C.I. tour at ceremonies at the United Nations, December 13.
"I started thinking of this seven years ago…new adventures, a broader series of inspirations, having grown possibly too familiar with Europe. It's really a joint effort to share information with other countries and it will provide new incentives for my own work. It also provides me the opportunity to discuss and share the use of new materials with craftsmen from countries where the exhibition tours…We've also learned how to specialize in hurricanes, blizzards and insurance."

Public information material for R.O.C.I. states:
"The Rauschenberg Overseas Culture Interchange is a planned five-year traveling exhibition of art created by world renowned artist Robert Rauschenberg. R.O.C.I. represents a longtime commitment of Mr. Rauschenberg to a project which he hopes to take to twenty-two nations. …R.O.C.I. consists of approximately 230 Rauschenberg works produced in the last two decades. The traveling exhibition will be enhanced and changed as works inspired by the cultural uniqueness of each country visited are developed…The artist's objective is to promote world peace and understanding through art. The exhibition will include painting, sculpture, drawings, prints, photographs, videos and sound that share with the world the environment, customs and noises of each country visited…The final show, to be held at the National Gallery in Washington, D.C., will be a celebration of the differences and similarities of as much of the world as R.O.C.I. and Mr. Rauschenberg are able to touch."

Receives Grammy Award, National Academy of Recording Arts and Sciences for Best Album Package, a commission for the cover of the limited edition version of Talking Heads' *Speaking in Tongues*.

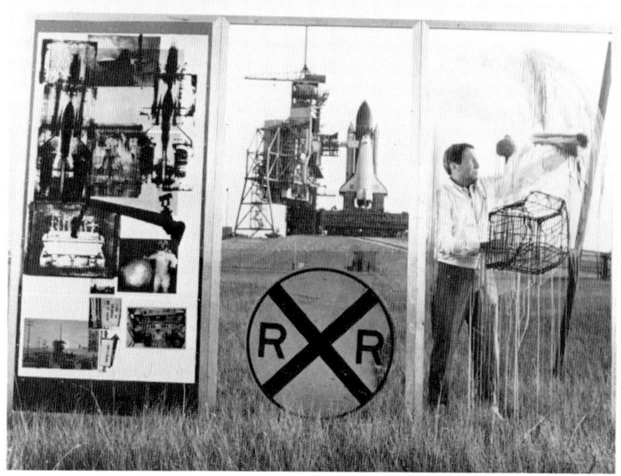

Robert Rauschenberg frames the space shuttle Discovery on its launch pad, in a work-in-progress, August 1984.

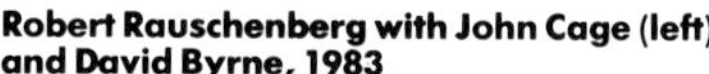

Robert Rauschenberg with John Cage (left) and David Byrne, 1983

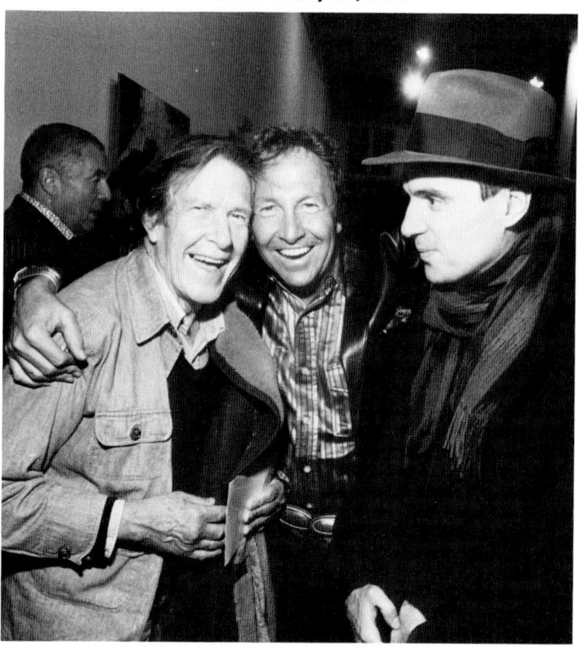

Receives Certificate of Appreciation from the United
Nations Committee Against Apartheid, for contribu-
tion of a poster design to the International Campaign
Against Apartheid in South Africa.

Awarded honorary doctorate of fine arts, New York
University.

Receives Jerusalem Prize for Arts and Letters. Friends
of the Bezatel Academy of Jerusalem, Philadelphia
chapter.

1985

Continues "Kabal American Zephyr" and "Salvage"
series. Begins work inspired by countries to which
R.O.C.I. has toured.

During 1985 the artist is primarily occupied by continued planning and research trips for R.O.C.I., install-
ing the exhibition at five locations and making new
works for each stop on the tour. Preparations continue
for touring the exhibition through 1989.

R.O.C.I. premiere exhibition, Museo Rufino Tamayo,
Mexico City.

R.O.C.I. at Museo Nacional de Bellas Artes, Santiago, Chile.

R.O.C.I. at Museo de Arte Contemporaneo de Caracas, Venezuela.

R.O.C.I. at National Art Gallery, Beijing, People's
Republic of China.

R.O.C.I. in Tibet, People's Republic of China.

Receives Andres Bello Medal for outstanding achieve-
ment in the fields of culture and education, presented
on behalf of Venezuela by President Jaime Lusinchi.

Receives Learning Disabled Achiever Award (for
overcoming dyslexia). Presented by The Lab School,
Washington, D.C., under the patronage of First Lady
Nancy Reagan.

*Robert Rauschenberg, Work from Four Series:
A Sesquicentennial Exhibition* opens in Houston,
December 21.

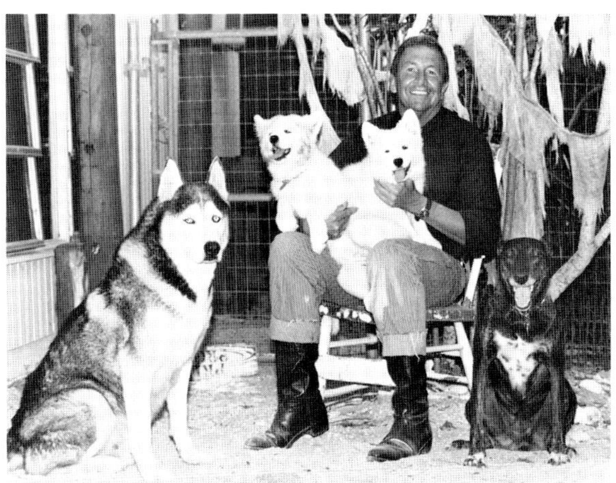

**Robert Rauschenberg at home on Captiva
Island with dogs, 1985**

Canary Stick (Cardboard) 1971
Cardboard on plywood support with wood pole
48 x 67¼", with 45"pole
Courtesy of the artist

**Lake Placid/Glori-Fried/Yarns from New England
(Cardboard)** 1971
Cardboard on plywood support with rope and wood pole
114¾ x 161 x 8"
Courtesy of the artist

Olympic/Lady Borden (Cardboard) 1971
Cardboard on plywood support
78 x 47½ x 12½"
Courtesy of the artist

Serita/Blister Pack (Cardboard) 1971
Cardboard mounted on plywood with insulated wire
and chamois
61½ x 49 x 47½"
Courtesy of the artist

Smash-Up (Cardboard) 1971
Mixed media on cardboard
Two panels, 32 x 42½" overall
Courtesy of the artist

Volon (Cardboard) 1971
Cardboard on plywood support
55½ x 147 x 10¾"
Courtesy of the artist

Groundings (Hoarfrost) 1974
Solvent transfer and collage on fabric
93 x 49"
Courtesy of the artist

Short Throttle (Hoarfrost) 1974
Solvent transfer and collage on fabric
103 x 40"
Courtesy of the artist

Spoke (Hoarfrost) 1974
Solvent transfer and collage on fabric
78 x 49¾"
Courtesy of the artist

Bologna Frost (Hoarfrost) 1975
Sewn fabric with cardboard collage
86½ x 49½"
Courtesy of the artist

Emerald (Hoarfrost) 1975
Solvent transfer and collage on fabric
92 x 36"
Courtesy of the artist

**Altar of the Infinite Lottery Winner
(Kabal American Zephyr)** 1981
Construction with solvent transfer, acrylic and collage
46½ x 40½ x 23¾"
Courtesy of the artist

The Ancient Incident (Kabal American Zephyr) 1981
Construction
86½ x 92 x 20"
Courtesy of the artist

**The Brutal Calming of the Waves by Moonlight
(Kabal American Zephyr)** 1981
Construction with acrylic
27 x 35½ x 85"
Courtesy of the artist

**Demons of Illness and Poverty Stalking the Lucky
Gods (Kabal American Zephyr)** 1981
Solvent transfer, acrylic and collage on wood veneer and
aluminum with objects
95 x 81 x 37¼"
Courtesy of the artist

**The Ghost of the Melted Bell
(Kabal American Zephyr)** 1981
Construction with acrylic
48¾ x 51½ x 66¾"
Collection Robert and Jane Meyerhoff, Phoenix, Maryland
(Houston only)

Greyhound Nightmare (Kabal American Zephyr) 1981
Solvent transfer, acrylic and collage on wood veneer and
aluminum with objects
56 x 88 x 97"
Collection Sydney Goldfarb

**The Lurid Attack of the Monsters from the Postal
News Aug. 1875 (Kabal American Zephyr)** 1981
Solvent transfer, acrylic and collage on wood veneer and
aluminum with objects
41 x 193 x 17¾"
Courtesy of the artist

**The Parade of the Wicked Thoughts of the Priest
(Kabal American Zephyr)** 1981
Solvent transfer, acrylic and collage on wood veneer with
objects
84 x 141 x 19"
Courtesy of the artist

**Petrified Relic from the Gyro Clinic
(Kabal American Zephyr)** 1981
Construction
42 x 19½ x 46"
Courtesy of the artist

The Proof of Darkness (Kabal American Zephyr) 1981
Construction
Dimensions variable
Courtesy of the artist

Sunflower Eclipse (Kabal American Zephyr) 1981
Construction with solvent transfer, acrylic and collage
72¾ x 78 x 18½"
Courtesy of the artist

Tree of Life Prune (Kabal American Zephyr) 1981
Construction with solvent transfer, acrylic and collage
53 x 52½ x 26"
Courtesy of the artist

Andy Boy Polka (Bifocal) 1982
(Double-faced)
Solvent transfer, acrylic and collage on cardboard
77½ x 25¼"
Courtesy of the artist

Garden Spot (Bifocal) 1982
(Double-faced)
Solvent transfer, acrylic and collage on cardboard
45 x 50½"
Collection Emil Fray

Ice Egg Metropole (Kabal American Zephyr) 1982
Construction
33¼ x 15 x 15"
Collection Roger I. Davidson, Toronto, Canada
(Houston only)

**The Interloper Tries To Hide His Disguises
(Kabal American Zephyr)** 1982
Solvent transfer and collage on wood veneer with objects
84½ x 76 x 61"
Courtesy of the artist

Lady Knight (Bifocal) 1982
(Double-faced)
Acrylic and collage on cardboard
29 x 24½"
Courtesy of the artist

Land + Sea Cross (Bifocal) 1982
(Double-faced)
Solvent transfer, collage and pencil on cardboard
46 x 43"
Courtesy of the artist

Live Fish Rush with Zappa (Bifocal) 1982
(Double-faced)
Solvent transfer, collage and acrylic on cardboard
68¼ x 33"
Collection Terry Van Brunt

Paper Riddle 1982
Collage and acrylic on cardboard
32½ x 33"
Collection Terry Van Brunt

Parrot Buckboard 1982
Solvent transfer, pencil and collage on cardboard
85¼ x 117"
Courtesy of the artist

**Pegasus' First Visit to America in the Shade of the
Flatiron Building (Kabal American Zephyr)** 1982
Solvent transfer, acrylic and collage on wood veneer and
aluminum with objects
96½ x 133½ x 22½"
Courtesy of the artist

Solar Elephant (Kabal American Zephyr) 1982
Solvent transfer, acrylic and collage on wood veneer and
aluminum with objects
104 x 83 x 15¾"
Courtesy of the artist

**The Vain Convoy of Europe Out West
(Kabal American Zephyr)** 1982
Solvent transfer, acrylic and collage on wood veneer with
objects
74 x 96½ x 41½"
Courtesy of the artist

Watermelon Medley (Bifocal) 1982
(Double-faced)
Solvent transfer, acrylic, collage and pencil on cardboard
93½ x 22½"
Courtesy of the artist

World's Stream Chart (Kabal American Zephyr) 1982
Solvent transfer and collage on wood veneer and aluminum
with objects
96¾ x 37⅛ x 25¾"
Courtesy of the artist

**Classic Cattleman Counter Column
(Late Kabal American Zephyr)** 1983
Construction
27 x 12½" diam.
Courtesy of the artist

Untitled (Late Kabal American Zephyr) 1985
Construction
73½ x 24 x 28¼"
Courtesy of the artist

*All dimensions are given in inches with height preceding
width and depth. The artist's term "construction" describes a
work composed of found objects.*

Plates

The following plates are arranged within series but do not necessarily appear in chronological order.

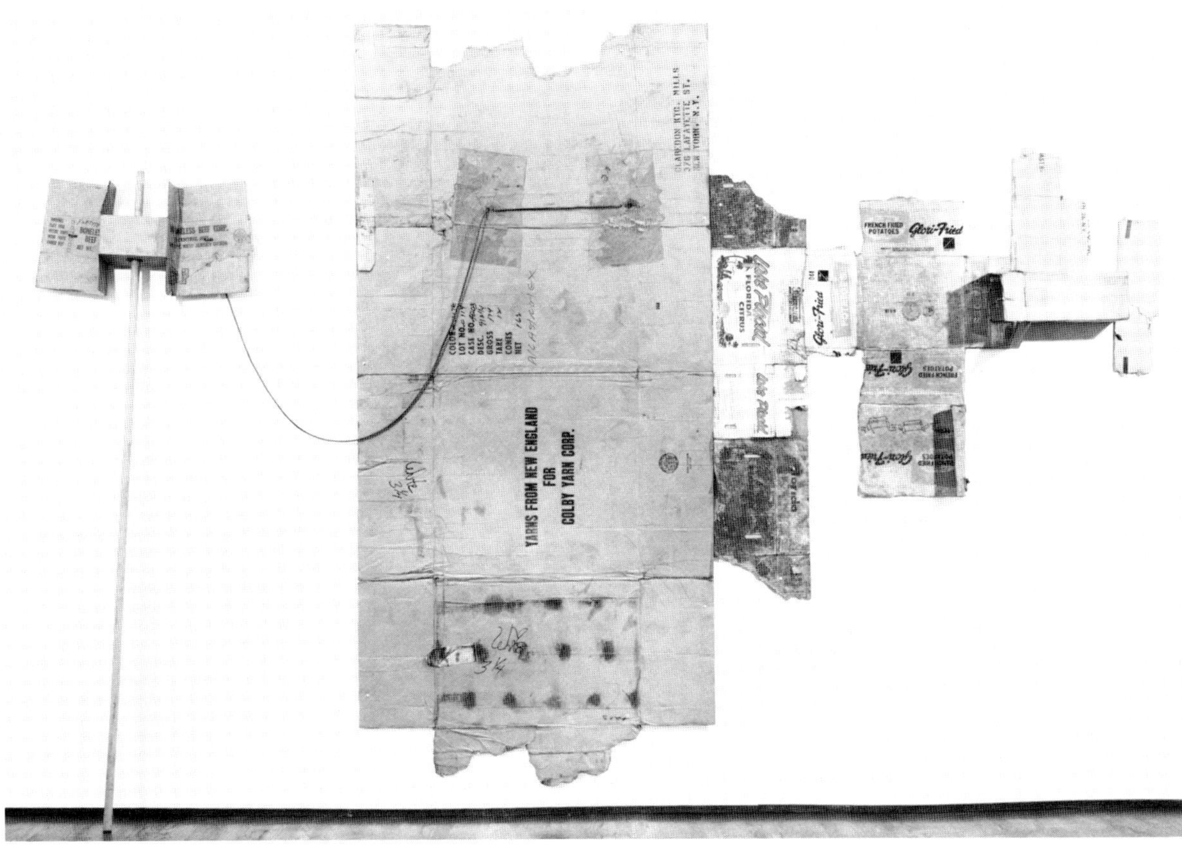

**Lake Placid/Glori-Fried/Yarns from New England
(Cardboard)** 1971
Cardboard on plywood support with rope and wood pole
114¾ x 161 x 8″
Courtesy of the artist

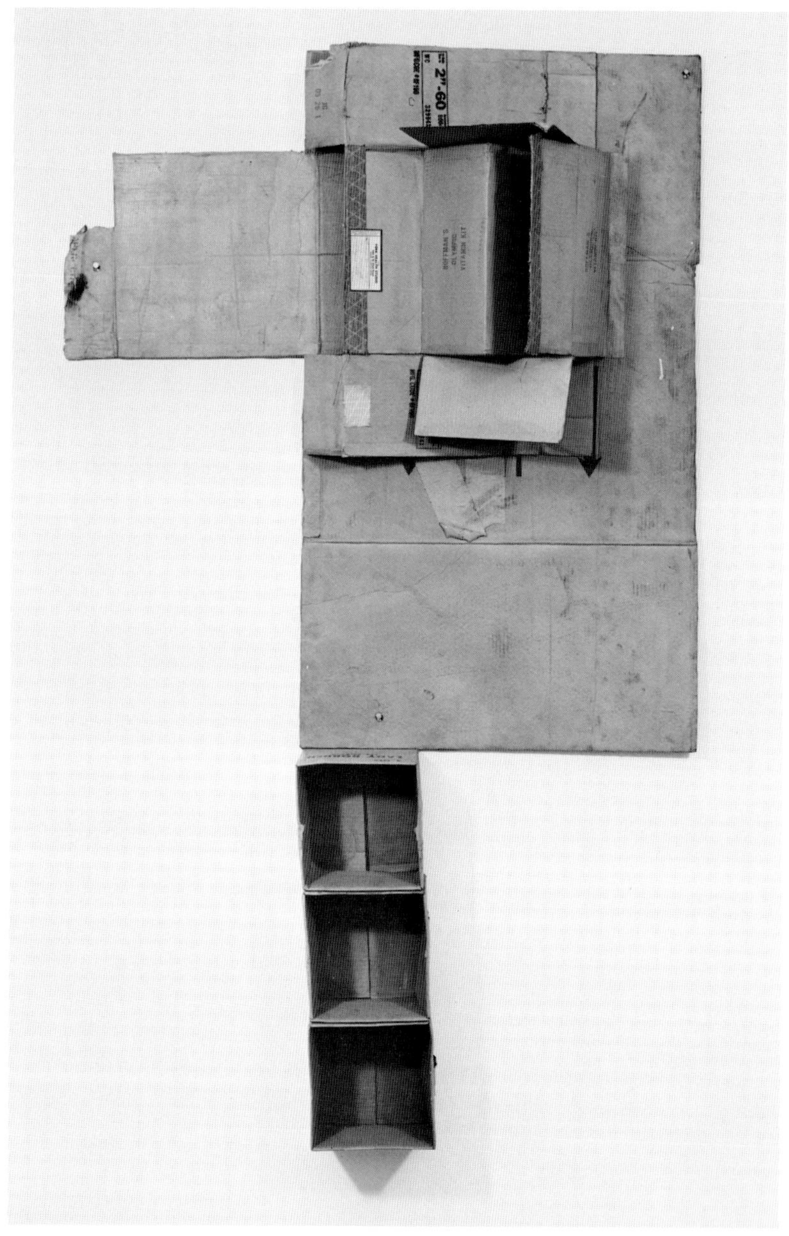

Olympic/Lady Borden (Cardboard) 1971
Cardboard on plywood support
78 x 47½ x 12½″
Courtesy of the artist

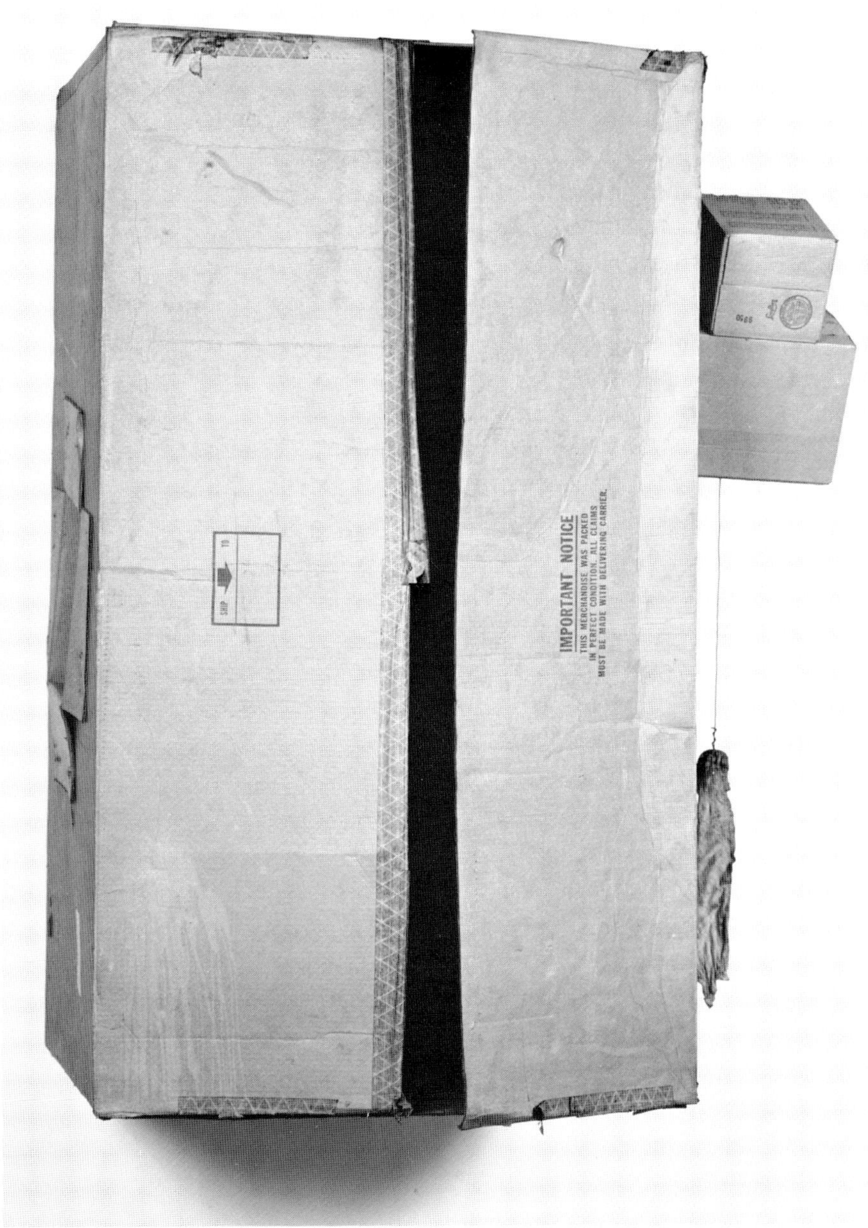

Serita/Blister Pack (Cardboard) 1971
Cardboard mounted on plywood with insulated wire
and chamois
61½ x 49 x 47½"
Courtesy of the artist

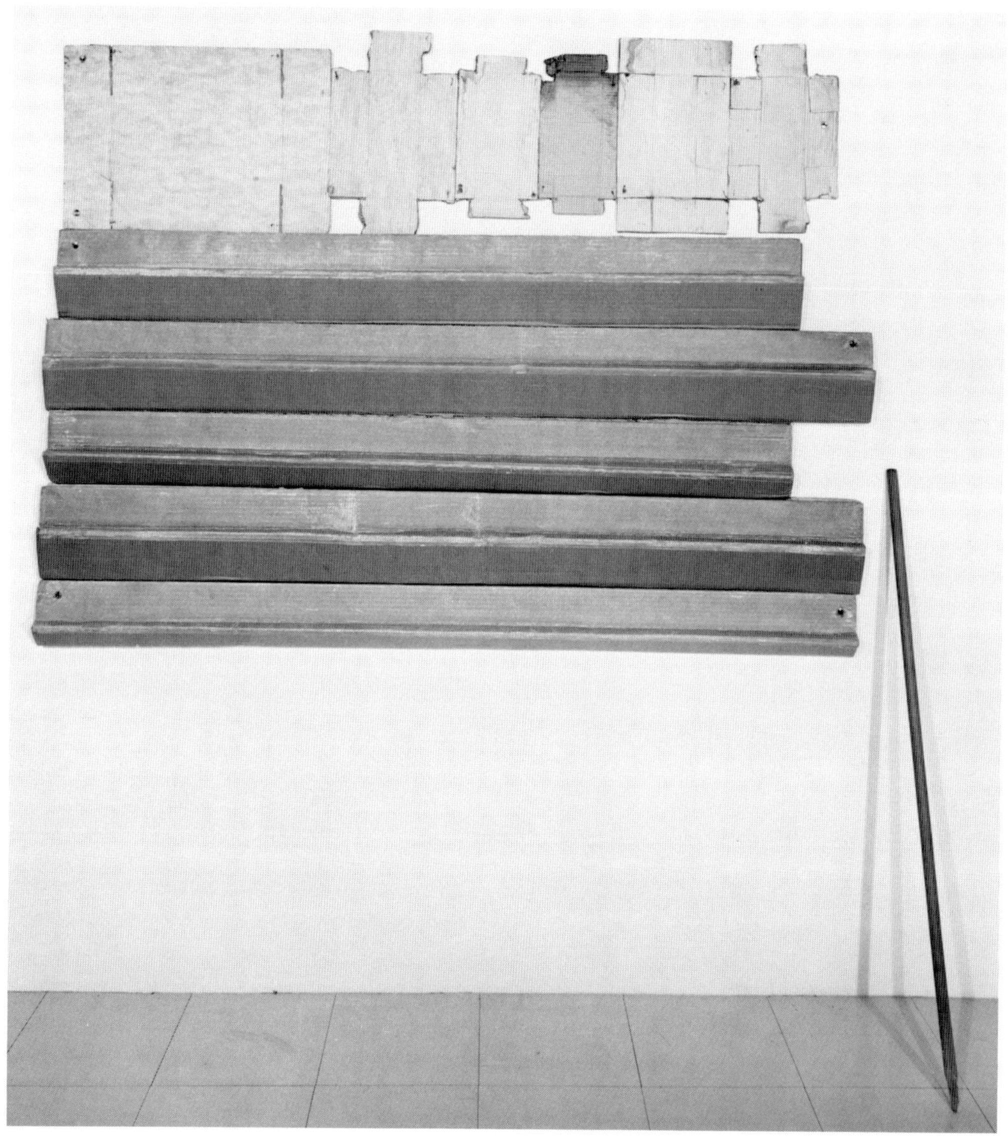

Canary Stick (Cardboard) 1971
Cardboard on plywood support with wood pole
48 x 67¼", with 45" pole
Courtesy of the artist

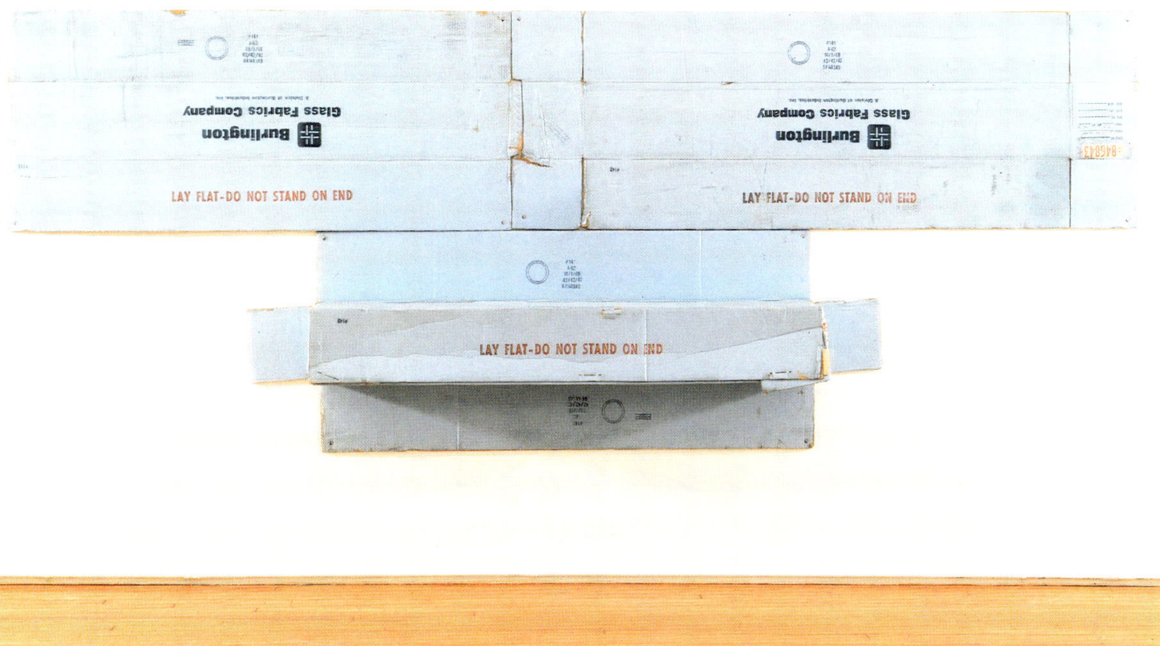

Volon (Cardboard) 1971
Cardboard on plywood support
55½ x 147 x 10¾″
Courtesy of the artist

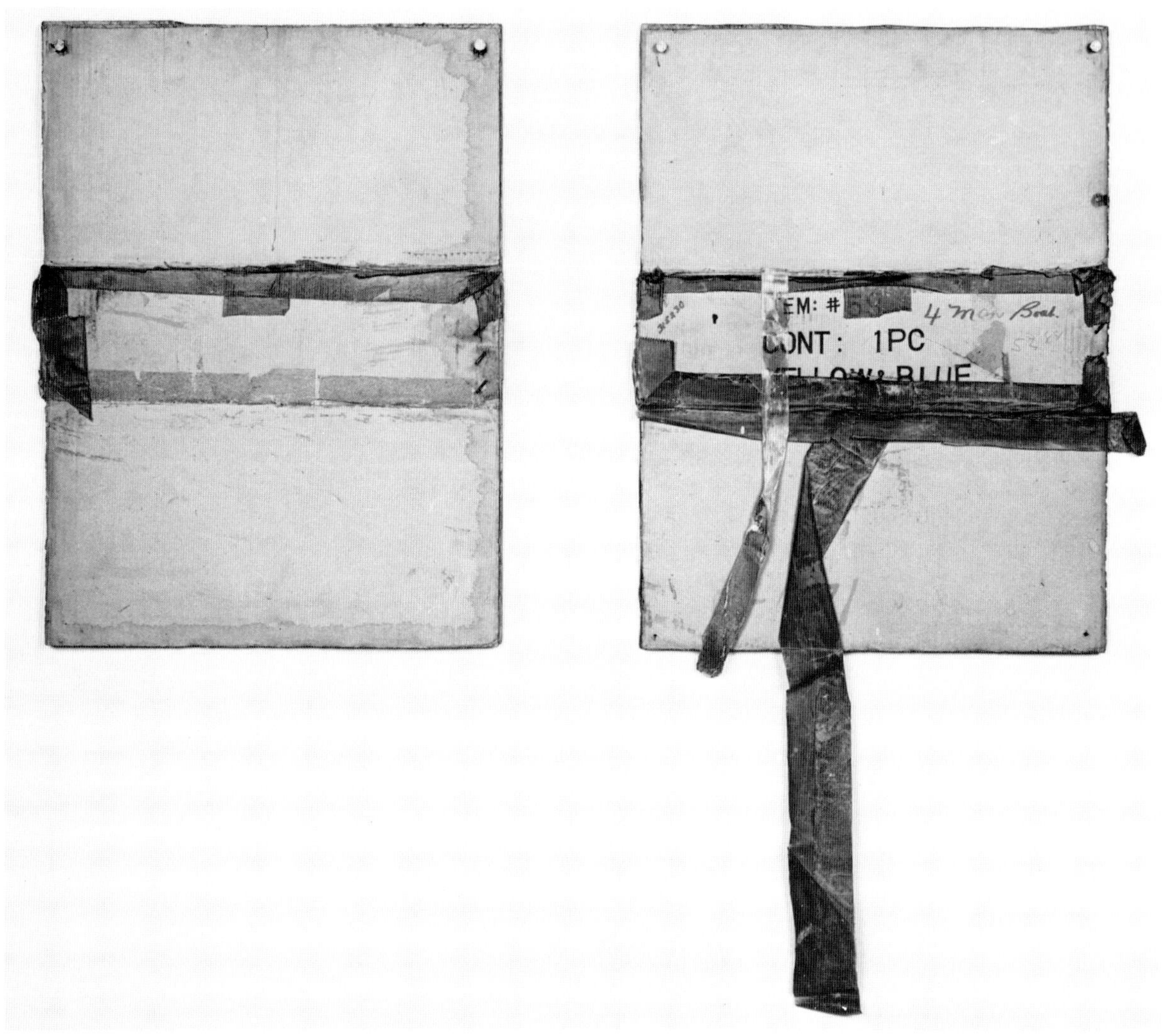

Smash-Up (Cardboard) 1971
Mixed media on cardboard
Two panels; 32 x 42½″ overall
Courtesy of the artist

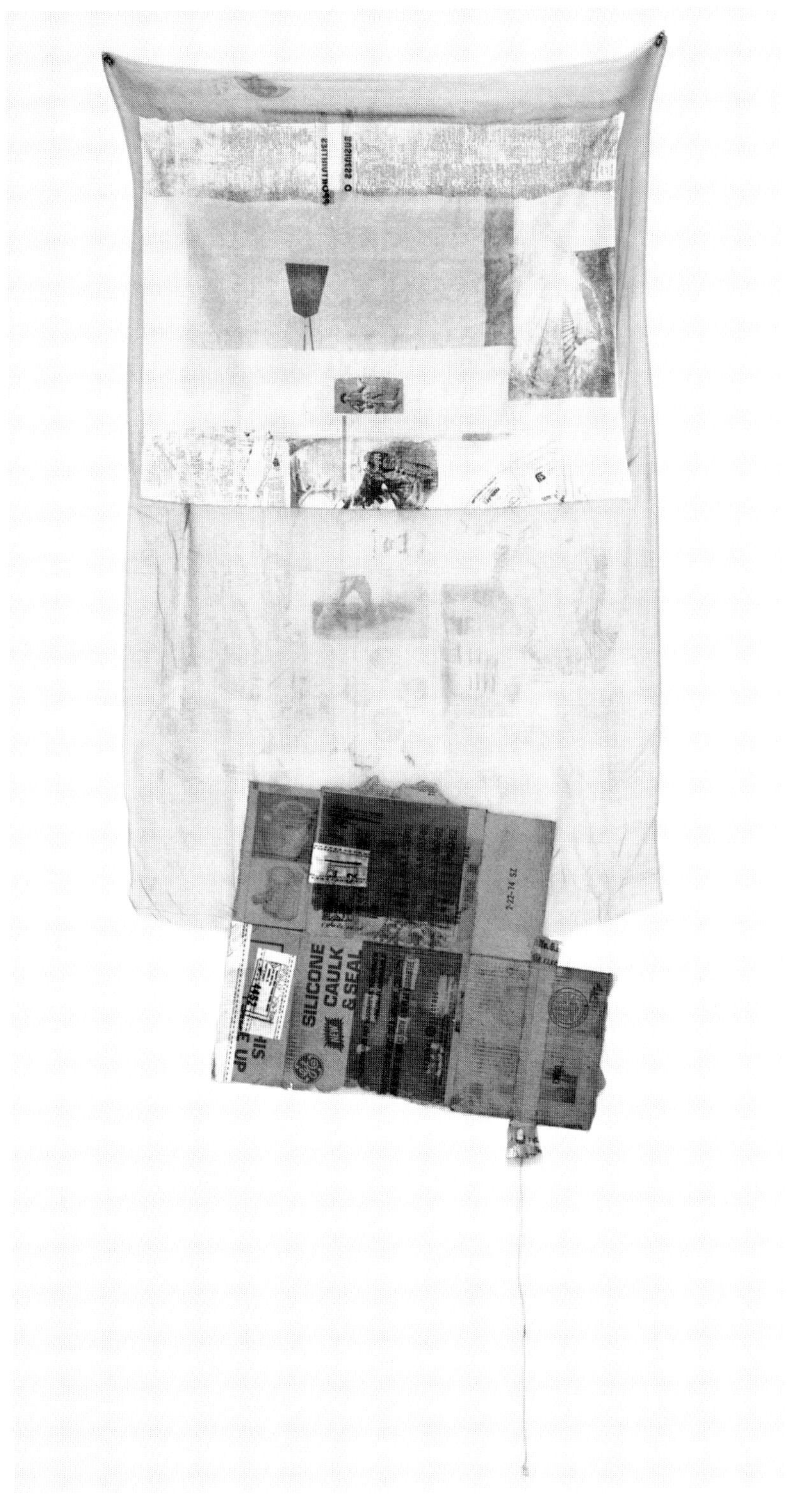

Short Throttle (Hoarfrost) 1974
Solvent transfer and collage on fabric
103 x 40″
Courtesy of the artist

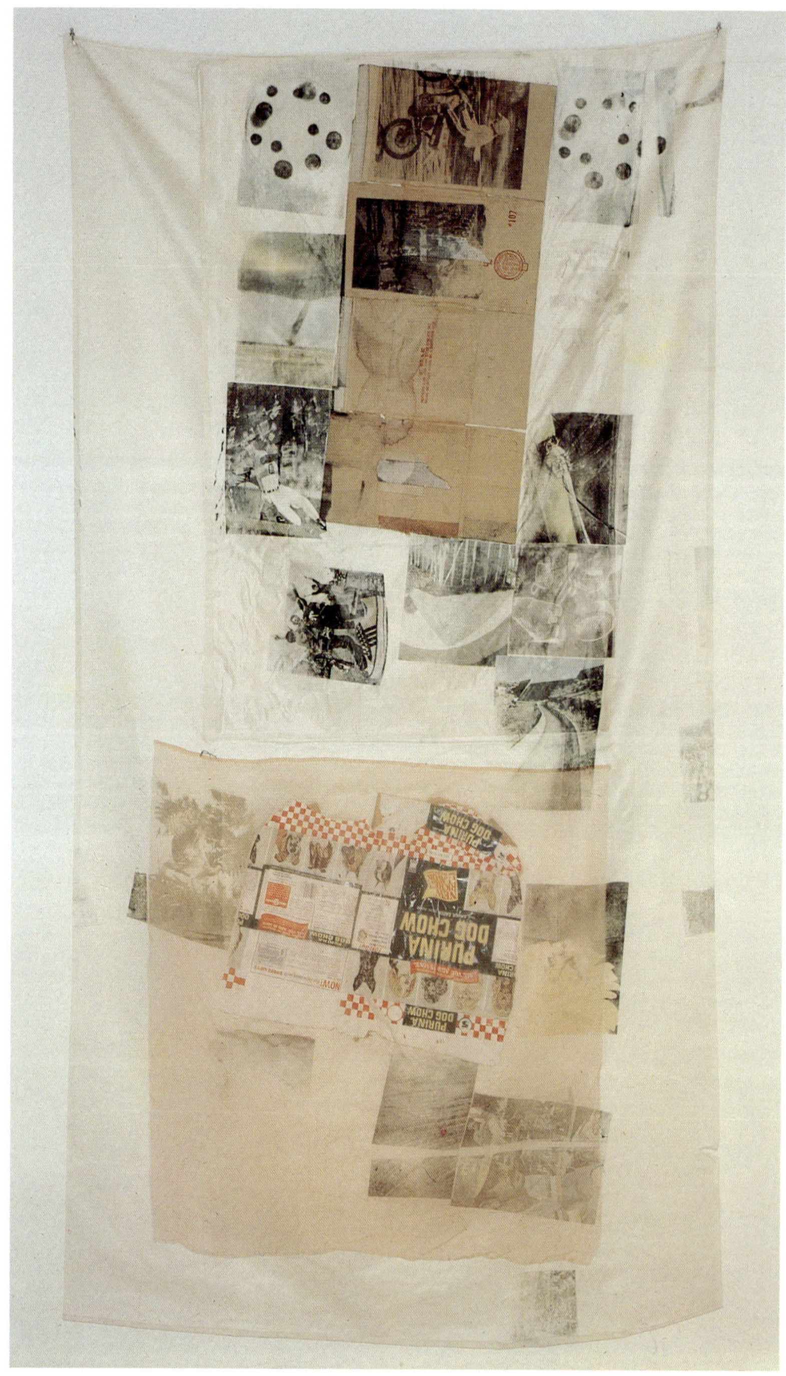

Groundings (Hoarfrost) 1974
Solvent transfer and collage on fabric
93 x 49″
Courtesy of the artist

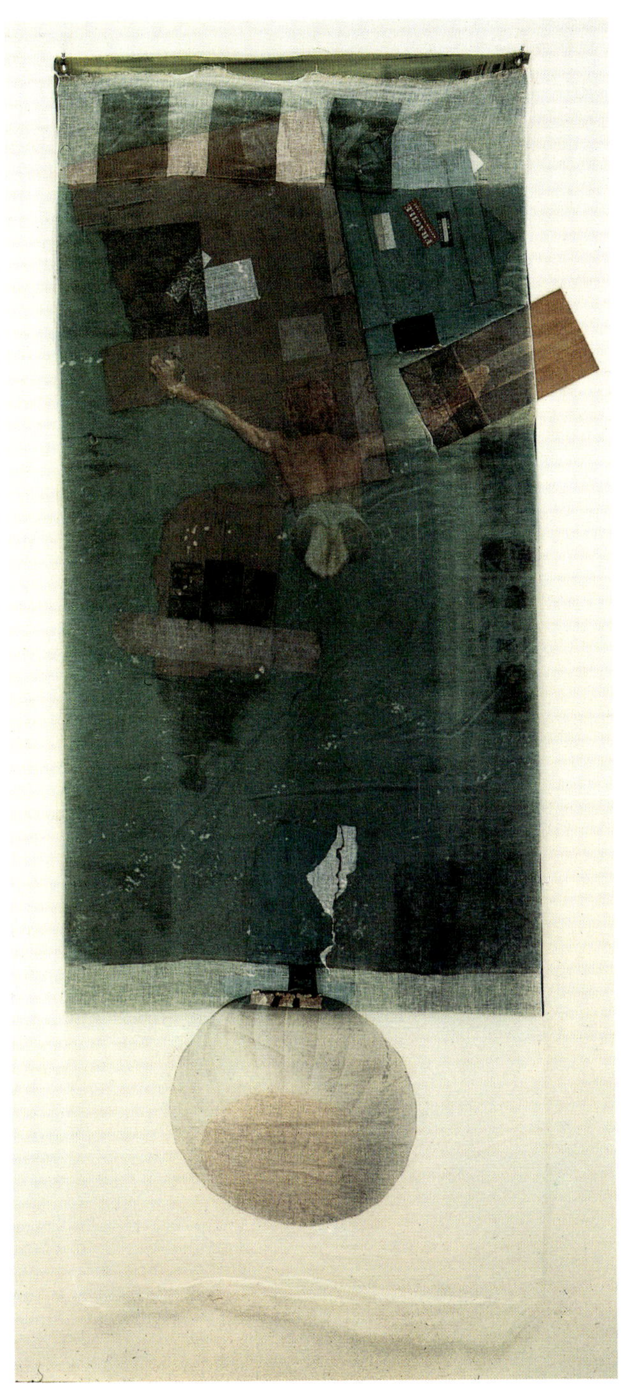

Emerald (Hoarfrost) 1975
Solvent transfer and collage on fabric
92 x 36″
Courtesy of the artist

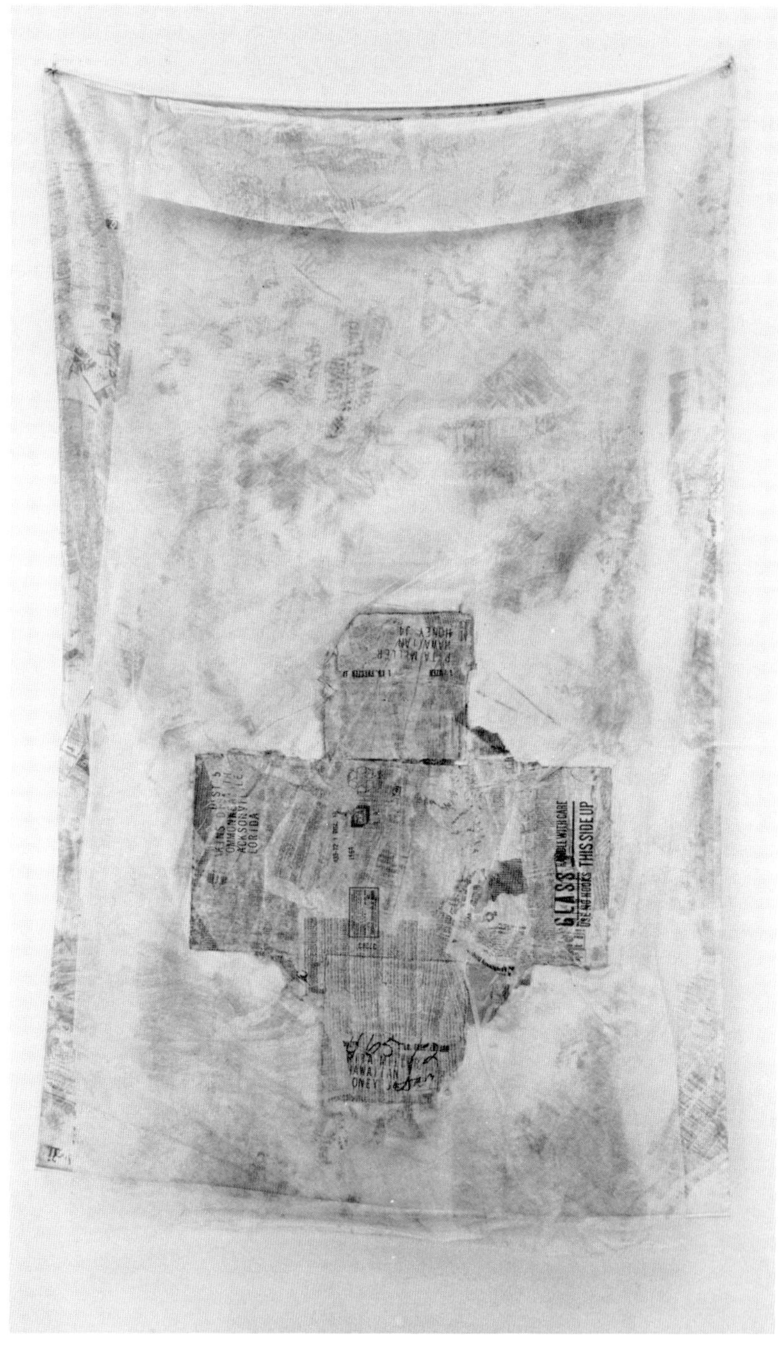

Spoke (Hoarfrost) 1974
Solvent transfer and collage on fabric
78 x 49¾"
Courtesy of the artist

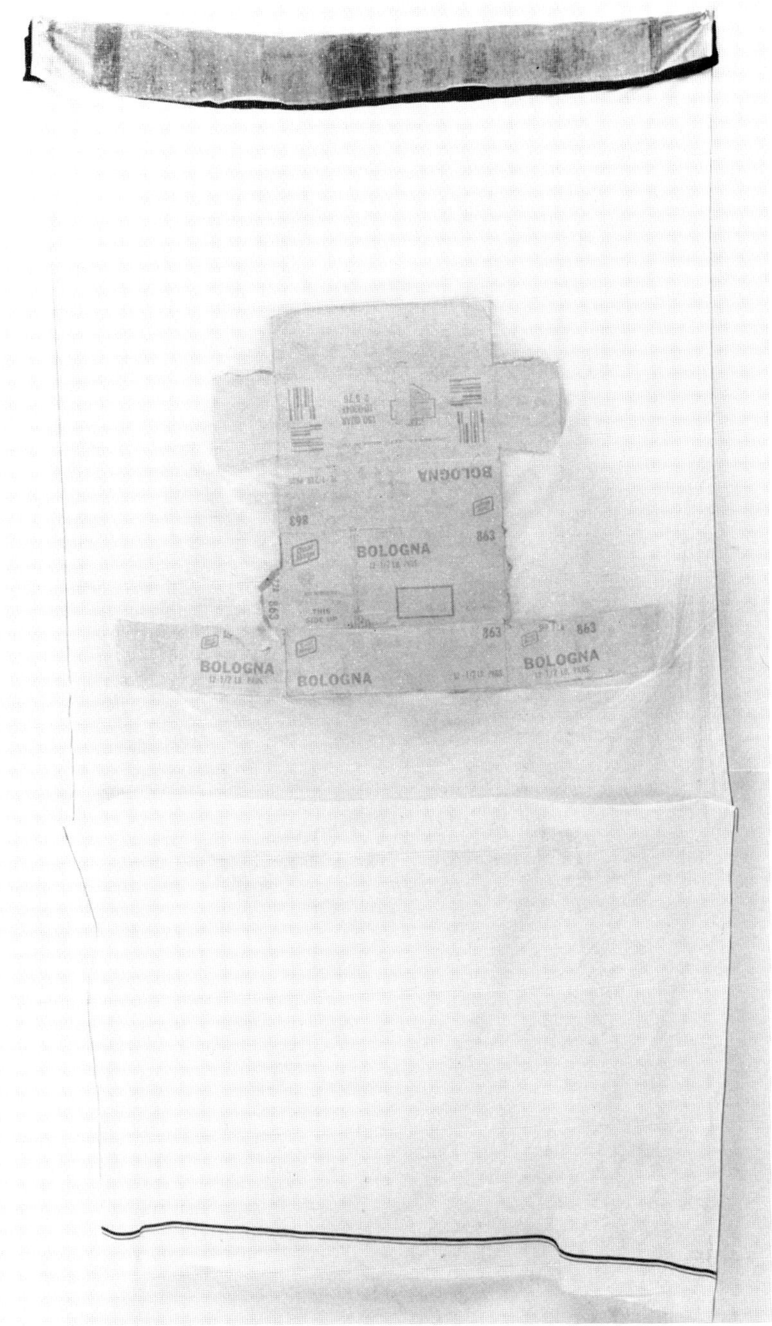

Bologna Frost (Hoarfrost) 1975
Sewn fabric with cardboard collage
86½ x 49½"
Courtesy of the artist

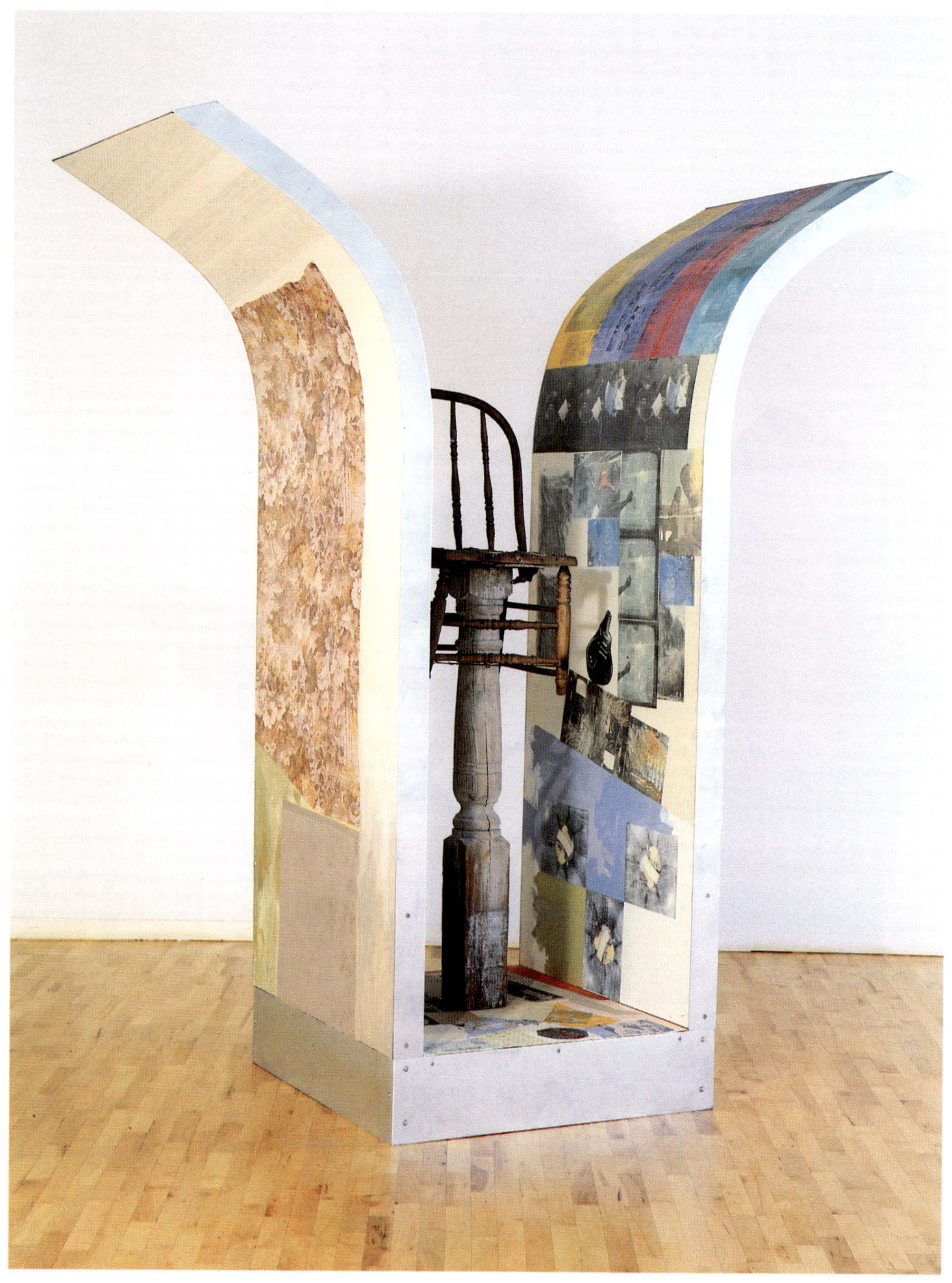

**Demons of Illness and Poverty Stalking the Lucky Gods
(Kabal American Zephyr)** 1981
Solvent transfer, acrylic and collage on wood veneer and
aluminum with objects
95 x 81 x 37¼″
Courtesy of the artist

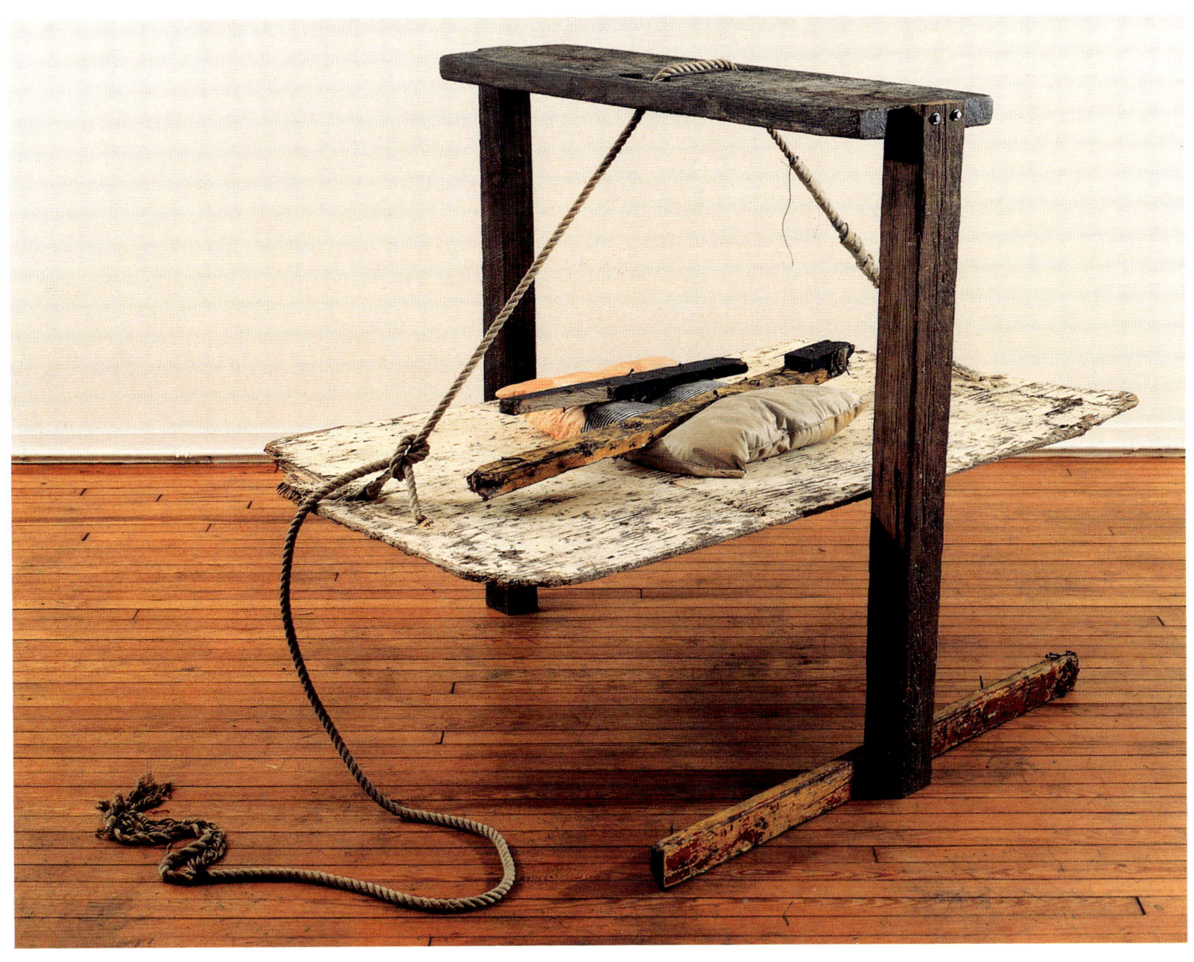

The Ghost of the Melted Bell
(Kabal American Zephyr) 1981
Construction with acrylic
48¾ x 51½ x 66¾"
Collection Robert and Jane Meyerhoff, Phoenix, Maryland

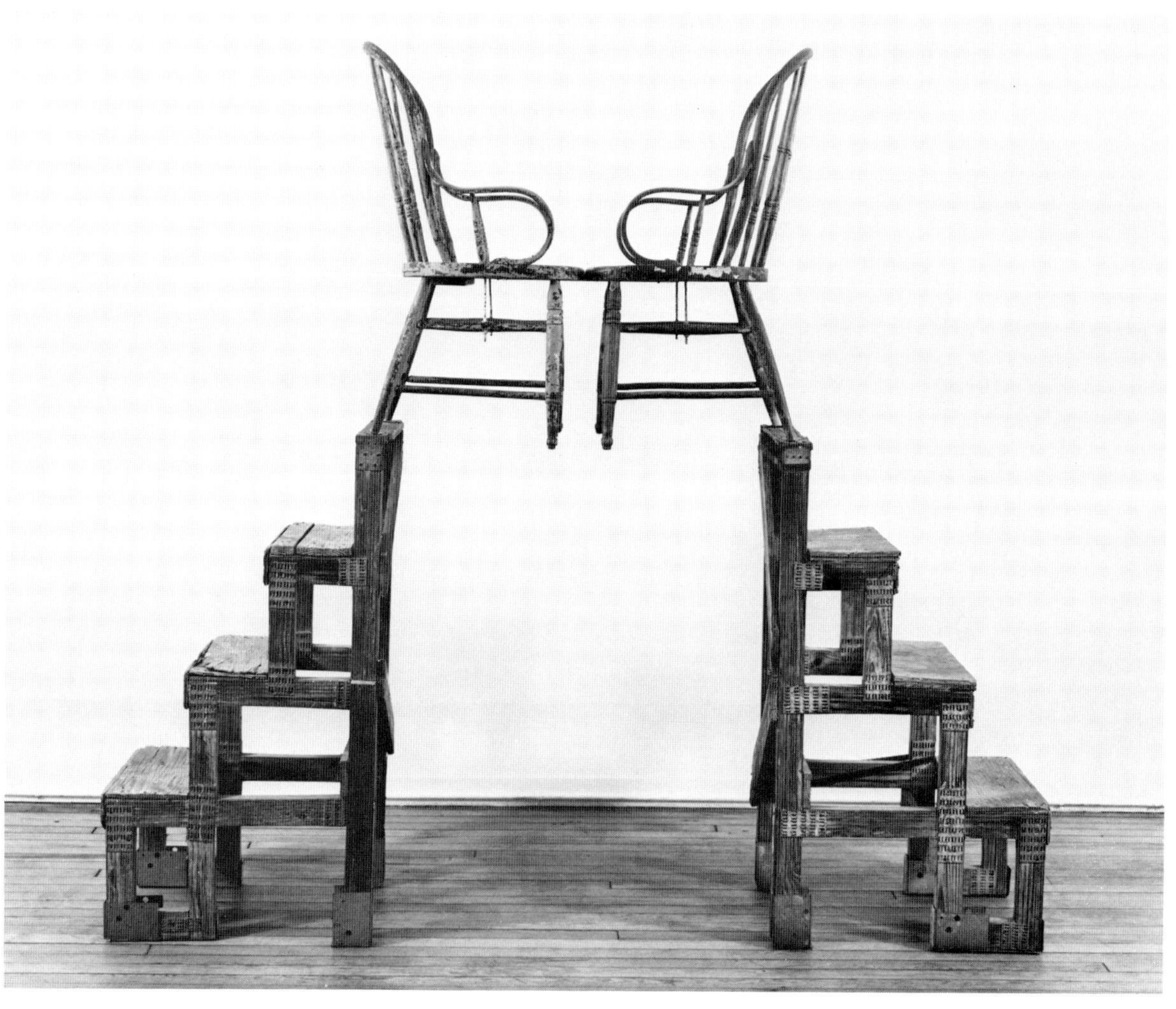

The Ancient Incident
(Kabal American Zephyr) 1981
Construction
86½ x 92 x 20″
Courtesy of the artist

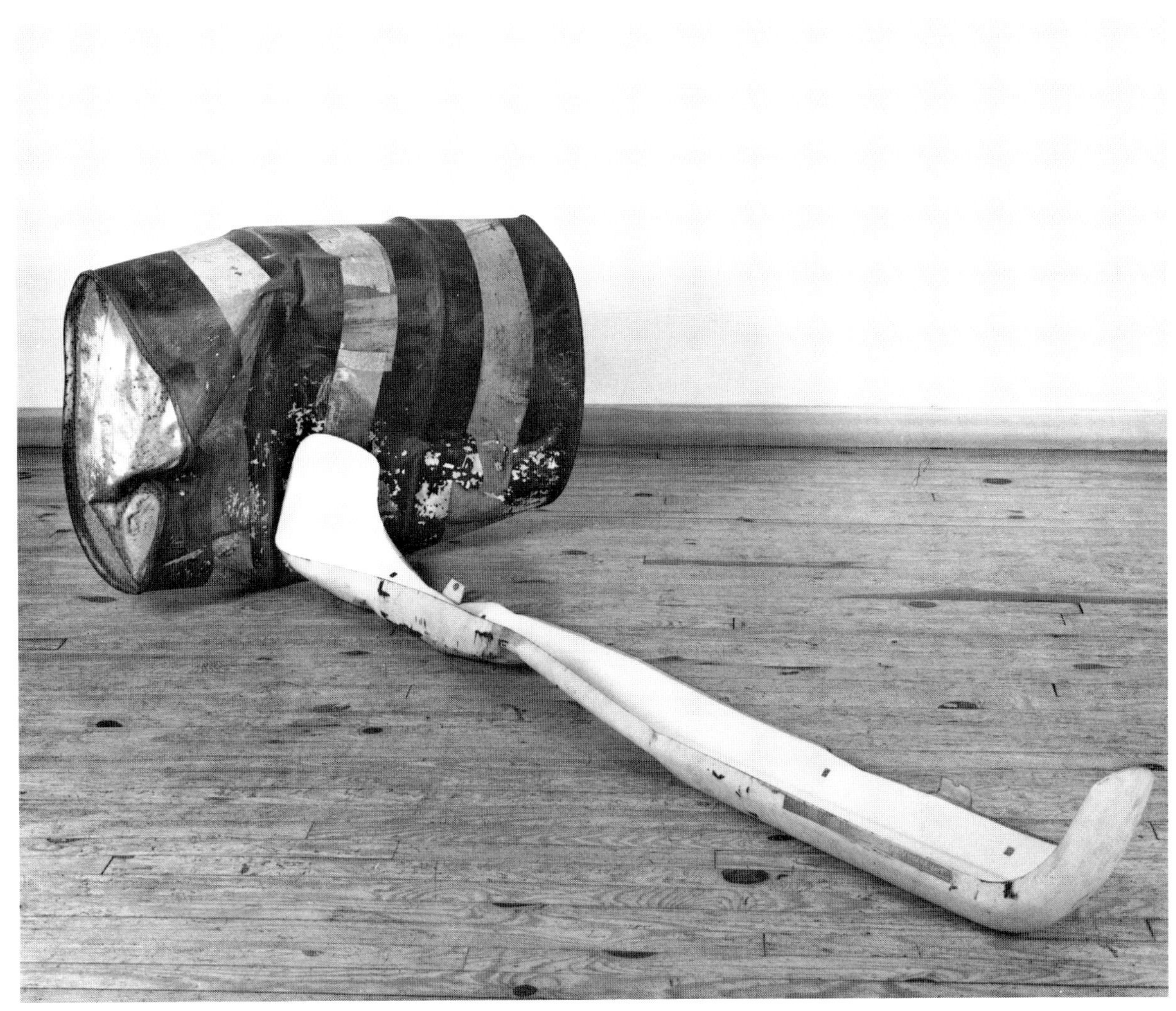

**The Brutal Calming of the Waves by Moonlight
(Kabal American Zephyr)** 1981
Construction with acrylic
27 x 35½ x 85″
Courtesy of the artist

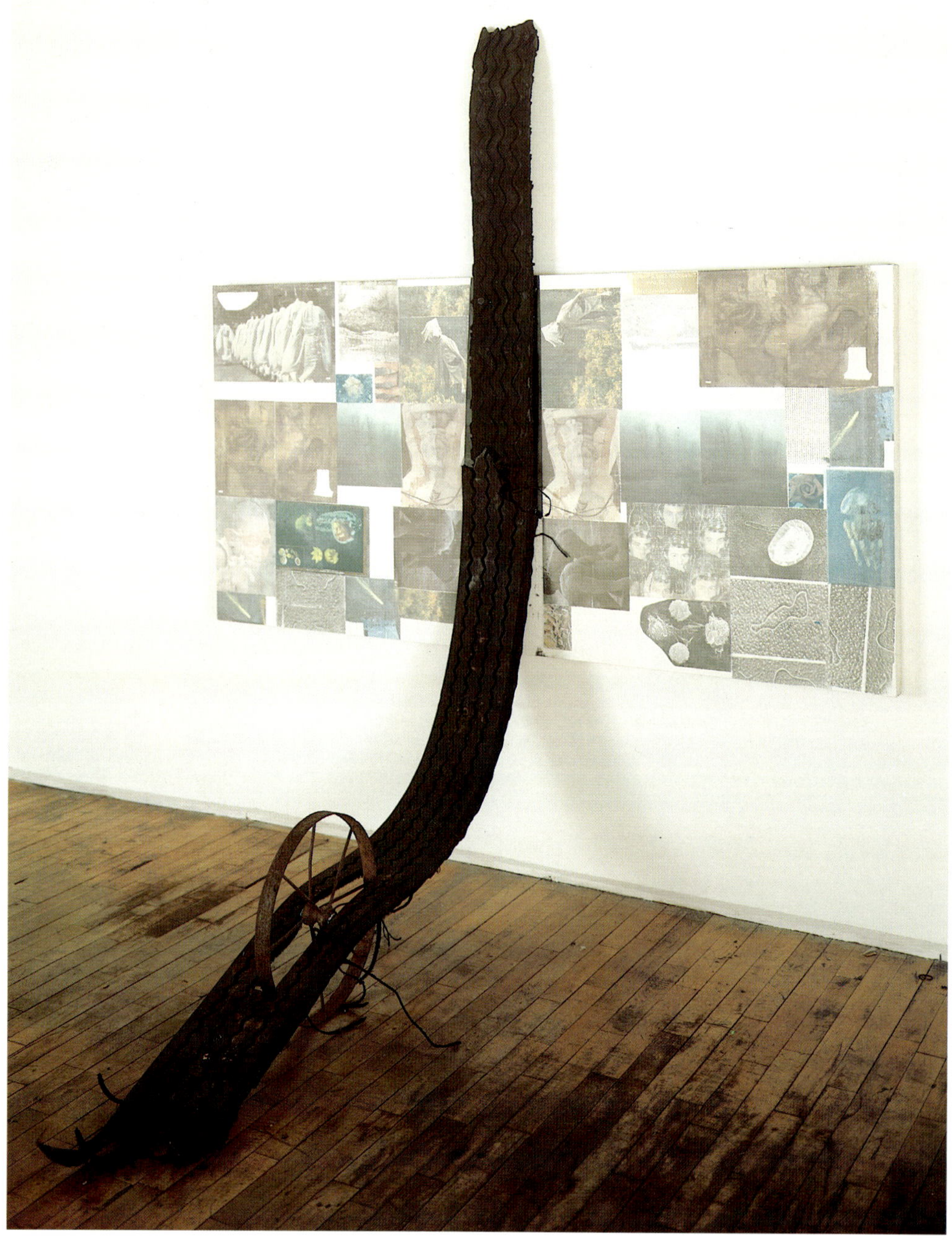

**The Interloper Tries To Hide His Disguises
(Kabal American Zephyr)** 1982
Solvent transfer and collage on wood veneer with objects
84½ x 76 x 61″
Courtesy of the artist

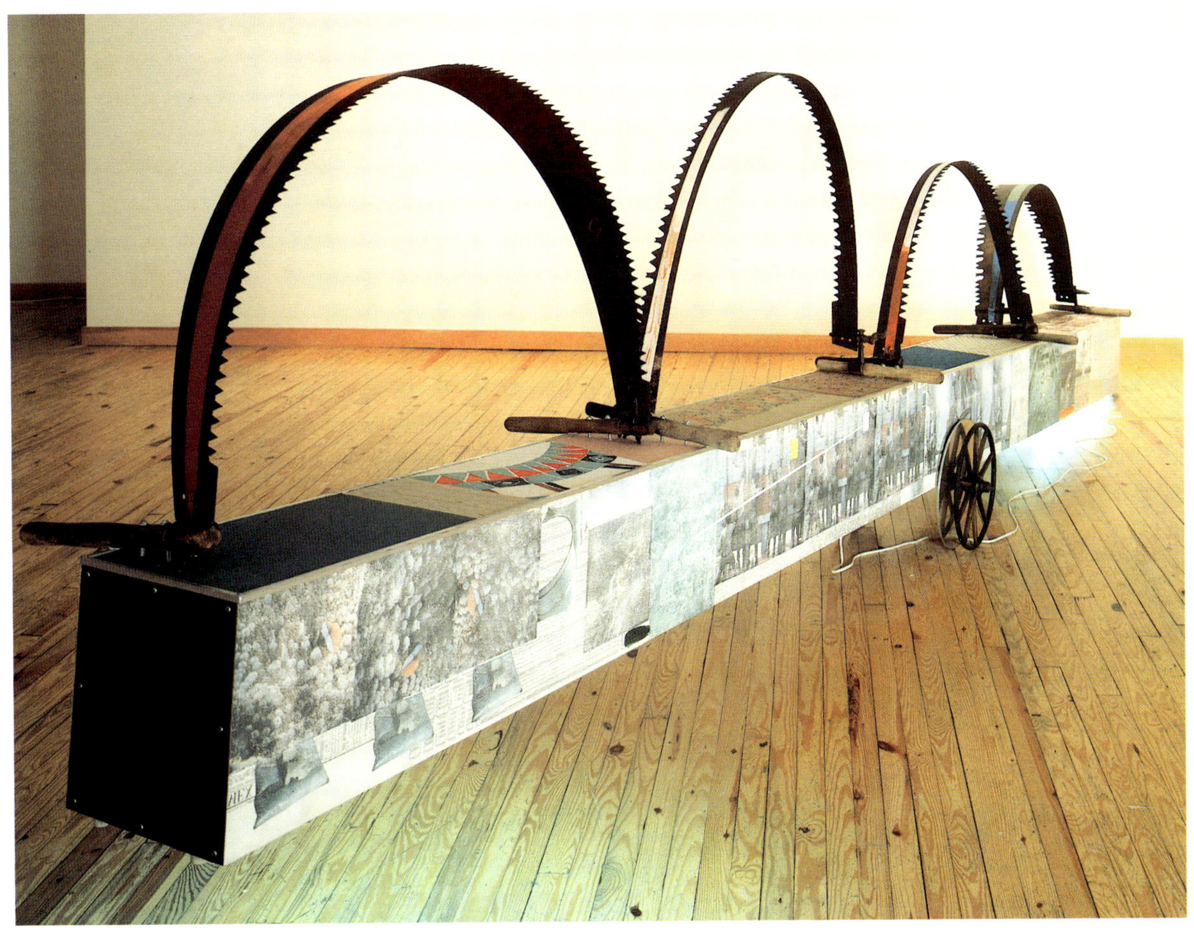

**The Lurid Attack of the Monsters from the Postal
News Aug. 1875 (Kabal American Zephyr)** 1981
Solvent transfer, acrylic and collage on wood veneer and
aluminum with objects
41 x 193 x 17¾″
Courtesy of the artist

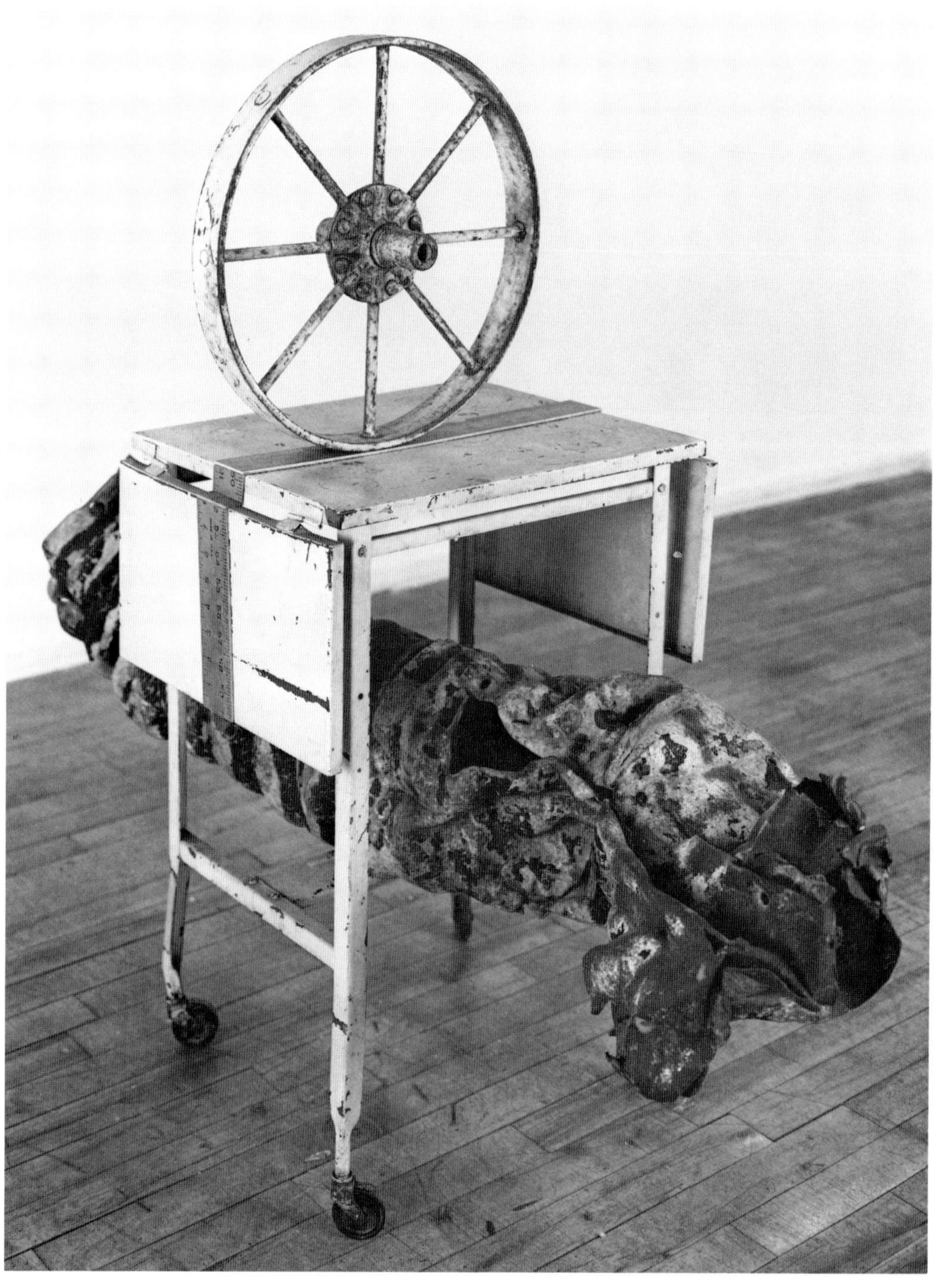

**Petrified Relic from the Gyro Clinic
(Kabal American Zephyr)** 1981
Construction
42 x 19½ x 46″
Courtesy of the artist

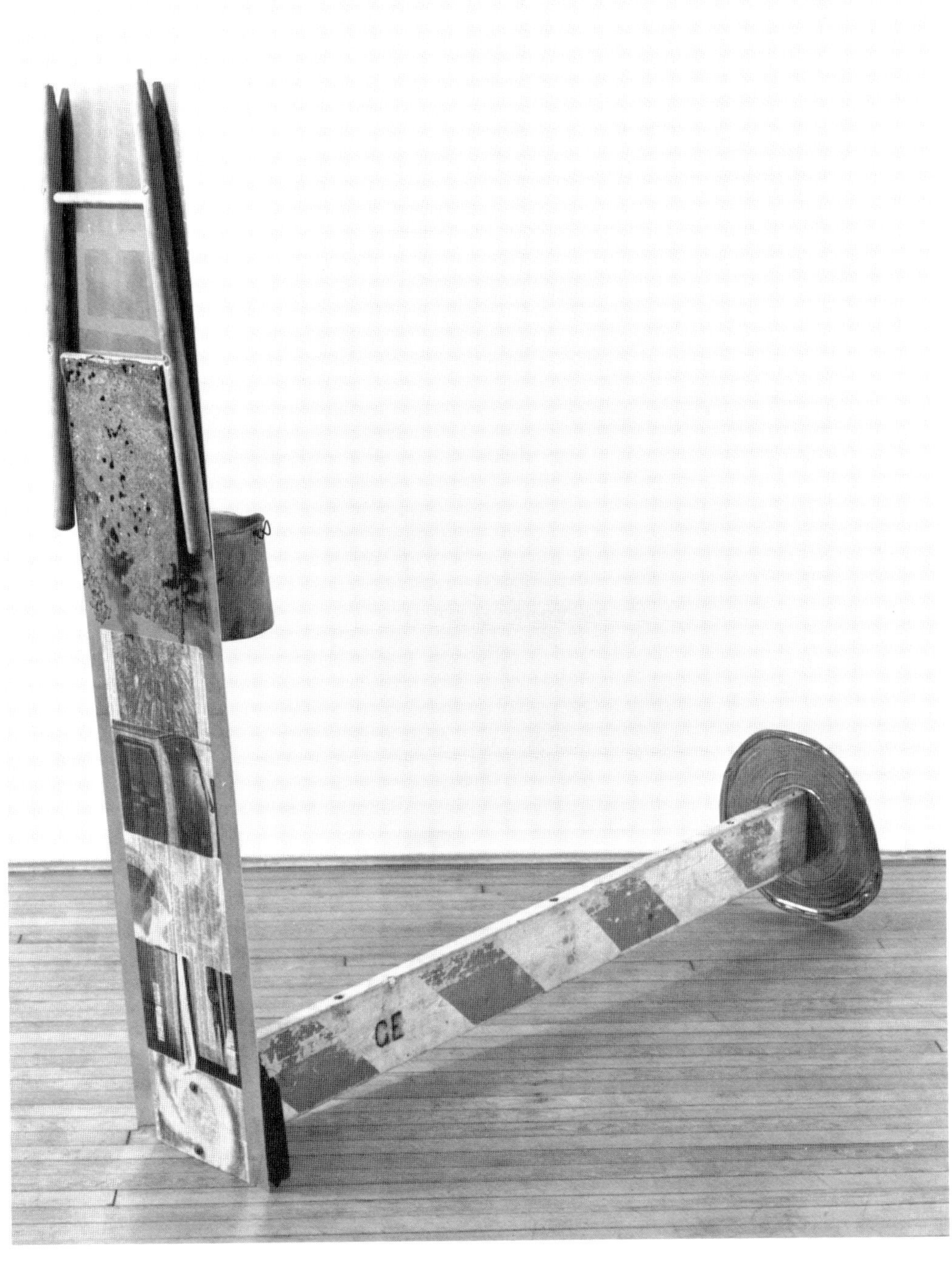

Sunflower Eclipse (Kabal American Zephyr) 1981
Construction with solvent transfer, acrylic and collage
72¾ x 78 x 18½″
Courtesy of the artist

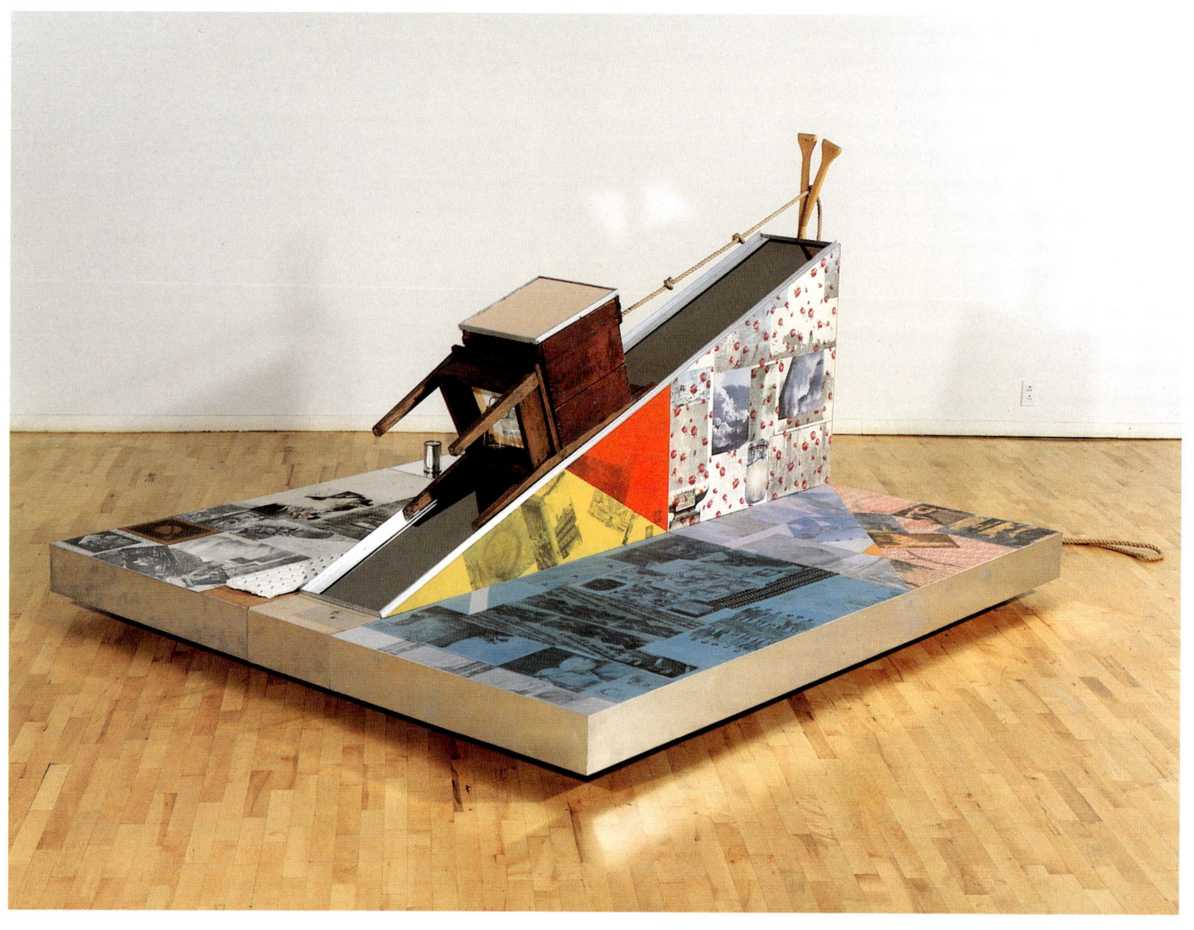

Greyhound Nightmare (Kabal American Zephyr) 1981
Solvent transfer, acrylic and collage on wood veneer and
aluminum with objects
56 x 88 x 97″
Collection Sydney Goldfarb

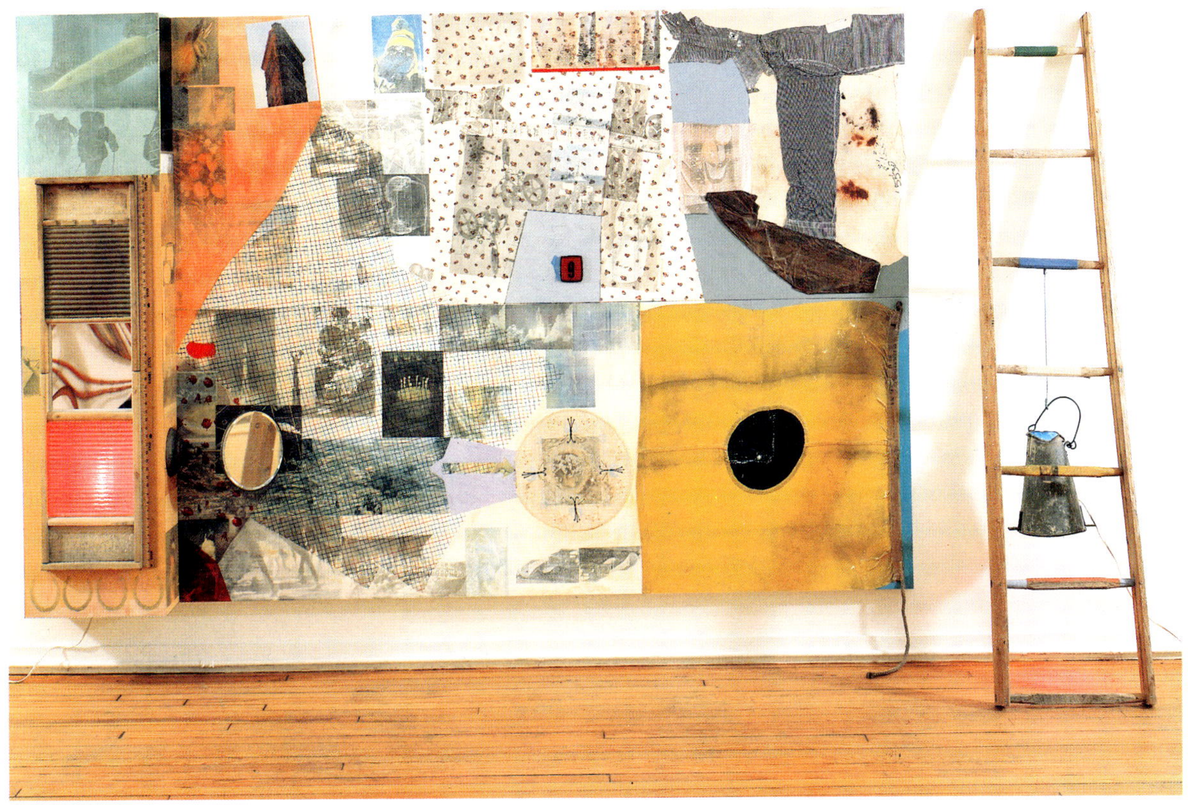

**The Parade of the Wicked Thoughts of the Priest
(Kabal American Zephyr)** 1981
Solvent transfer, acrylic and collage on wood veneer
with objects
84 x 141 x 19″
Courtesy of the artist

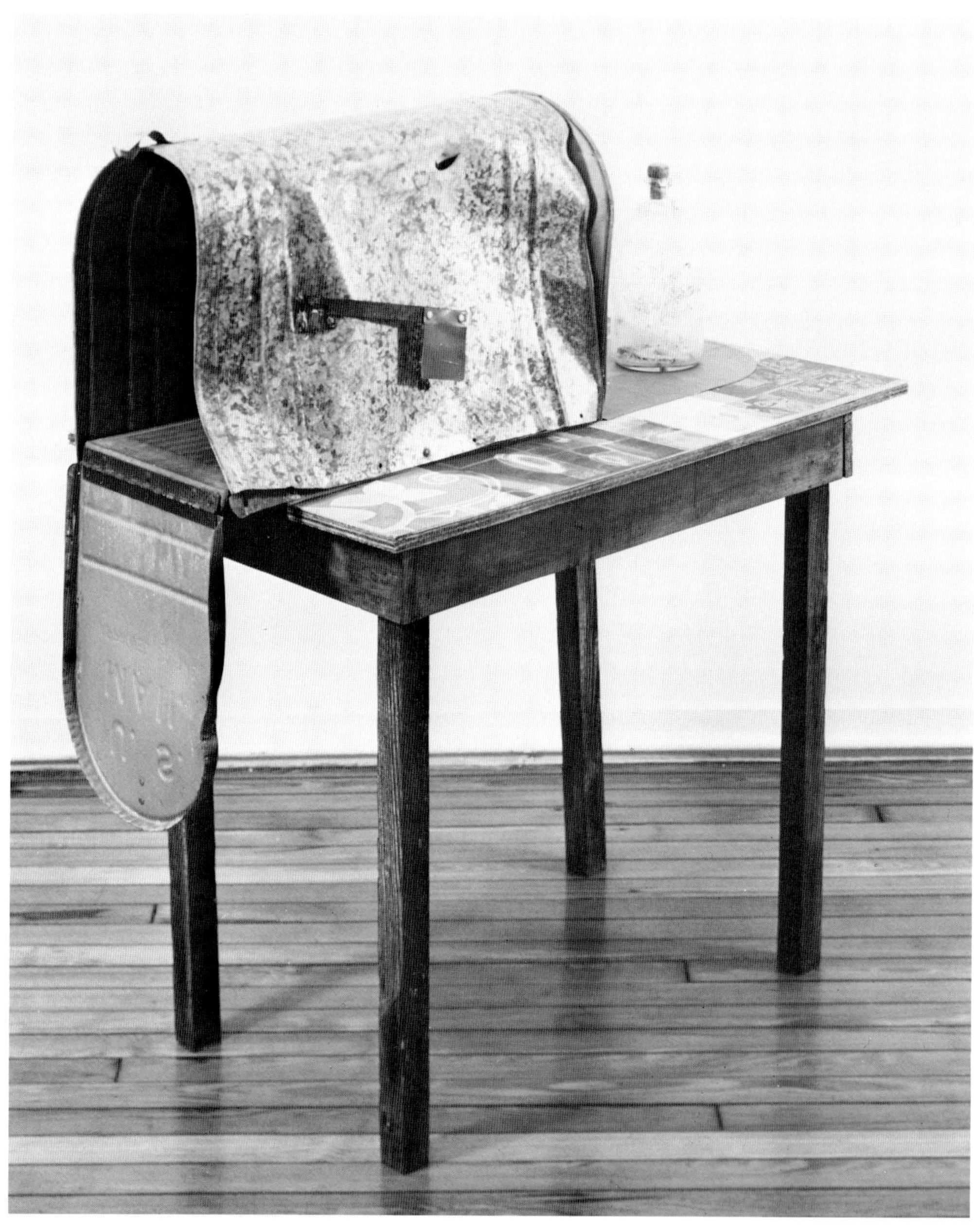

Altar of the Infinite Lottery Winner
(Kabal American Zephyr) 1981
Construction with solvent transfer, acrylic and collage
46½ x 40½ x 23¾″
Courtesy of the artist

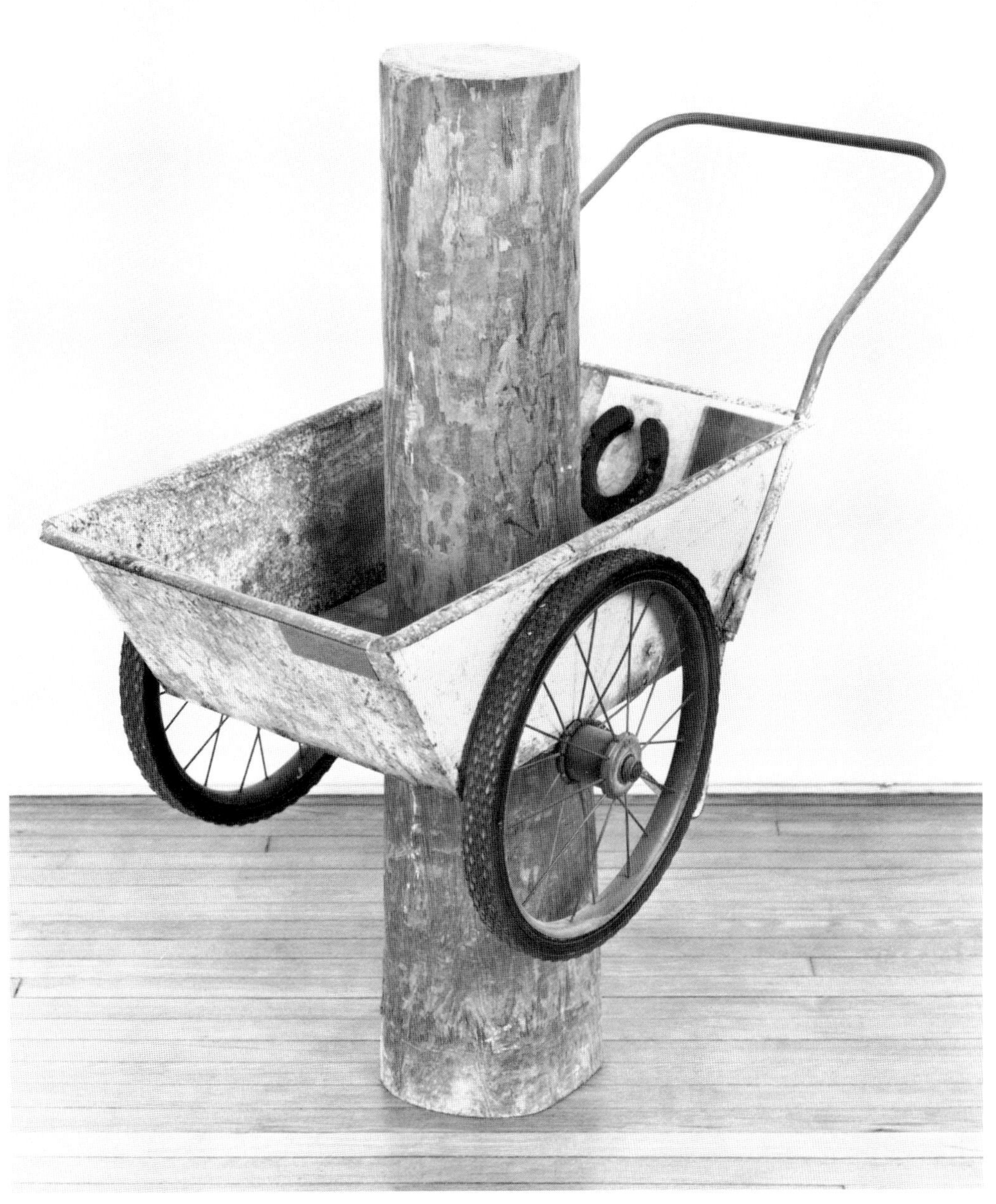

Tree of Life Prune (Kabal American Zephyr) 1981
Construction with solvent transfer, acrylic and collage
53 x 52½ x 26″
Courtesy of the artist

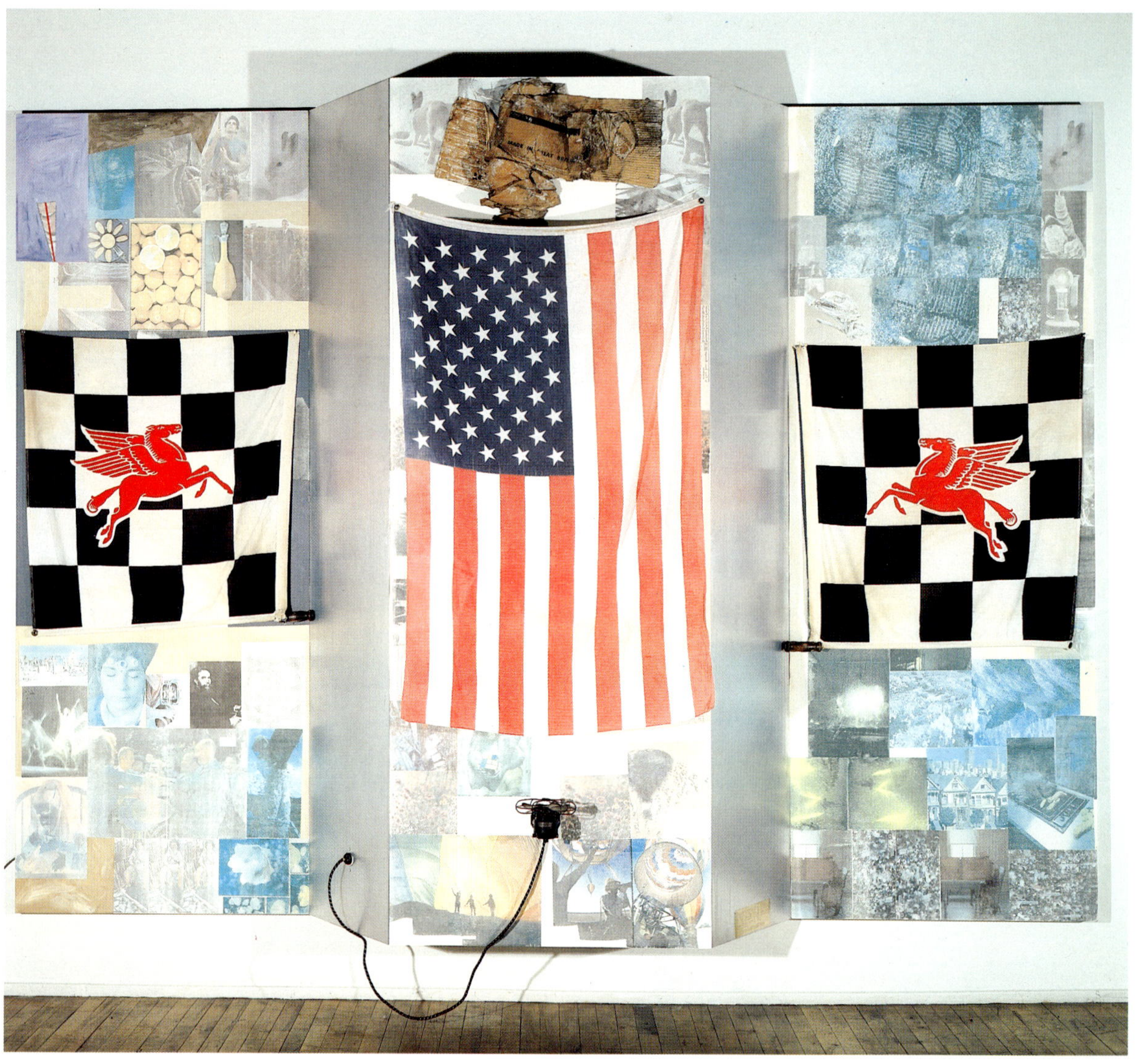

**Pegasus' First Visit to America in the Shade of the
Flatiron Building (Kabal American Zephyr)** 1982
Solvent transfer, acrylic and collage on wood veneer and
aluminum with objects
96½ x 133½ x 22½″
Courtesy of the artist

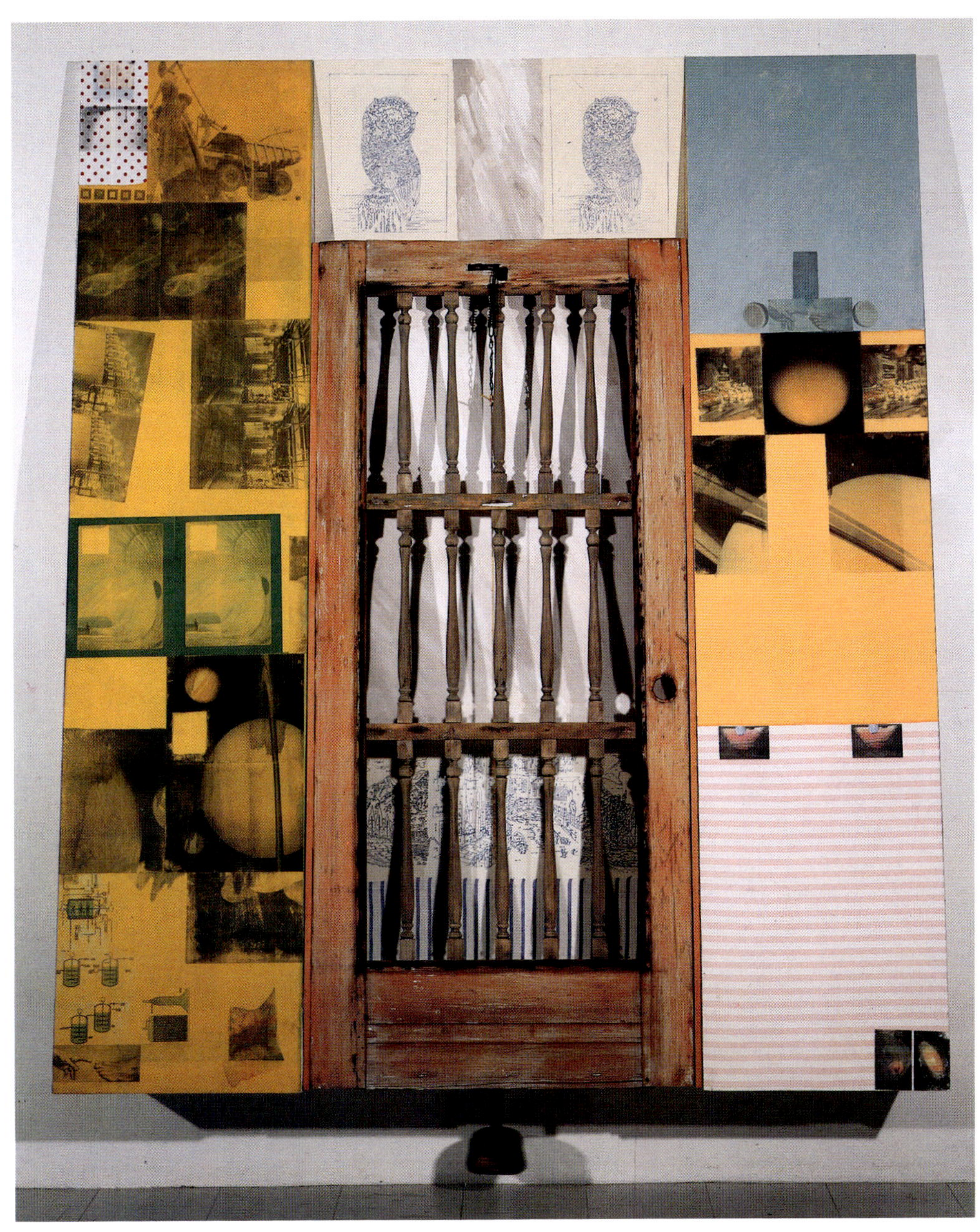

Solar Elephant (Kabal American Zephyr) 1982
Solvent transfer, acrylic and collage on wood veneer and
aluminum with objects
104 x 83 x 15¾″
Courtesy of the artist

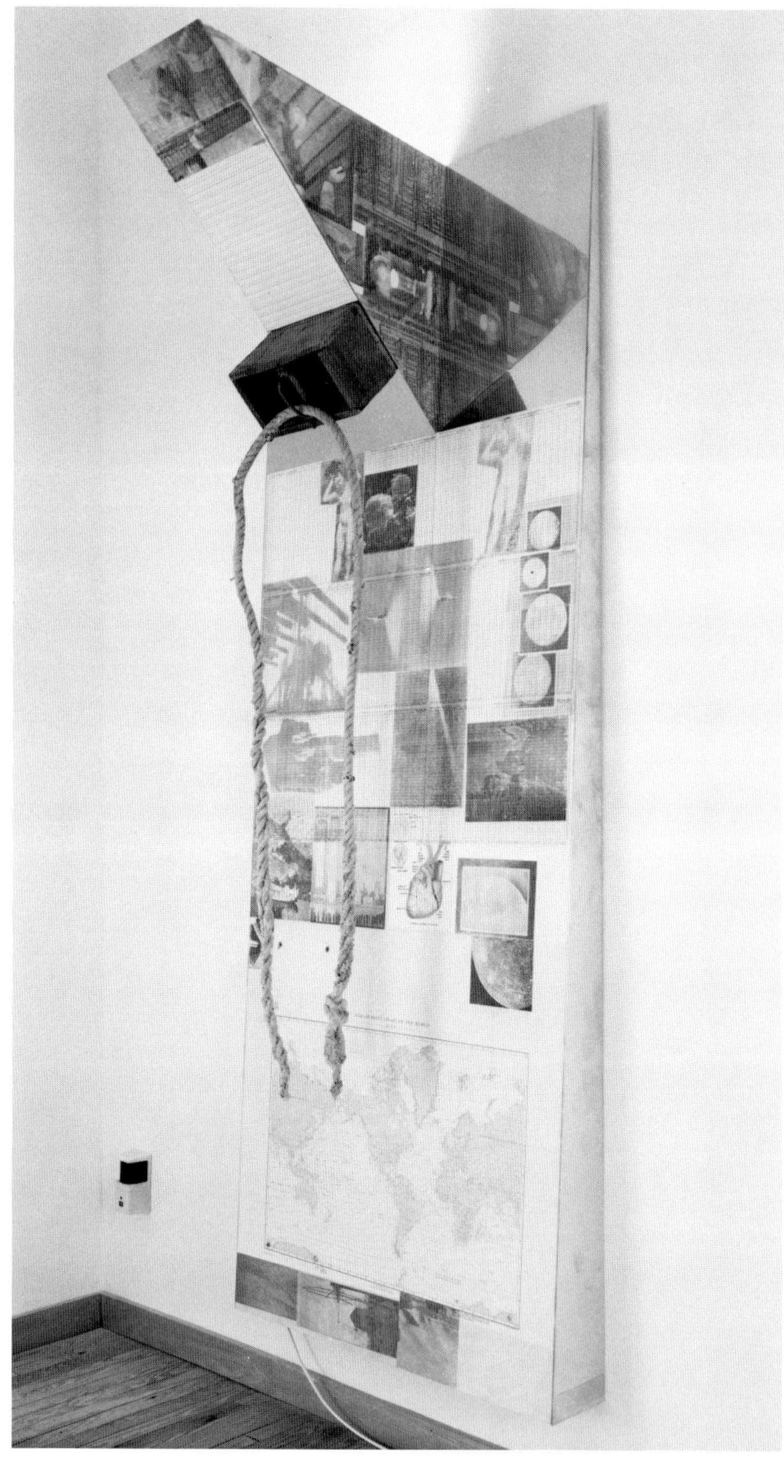

World's Stream Chart (Kabal American Zephyr) 1982
Solvent transfer and collage on wood veneer and aluminum
with objects
96¾ x 37⅛ x 25¾"
Courtesy of the artist

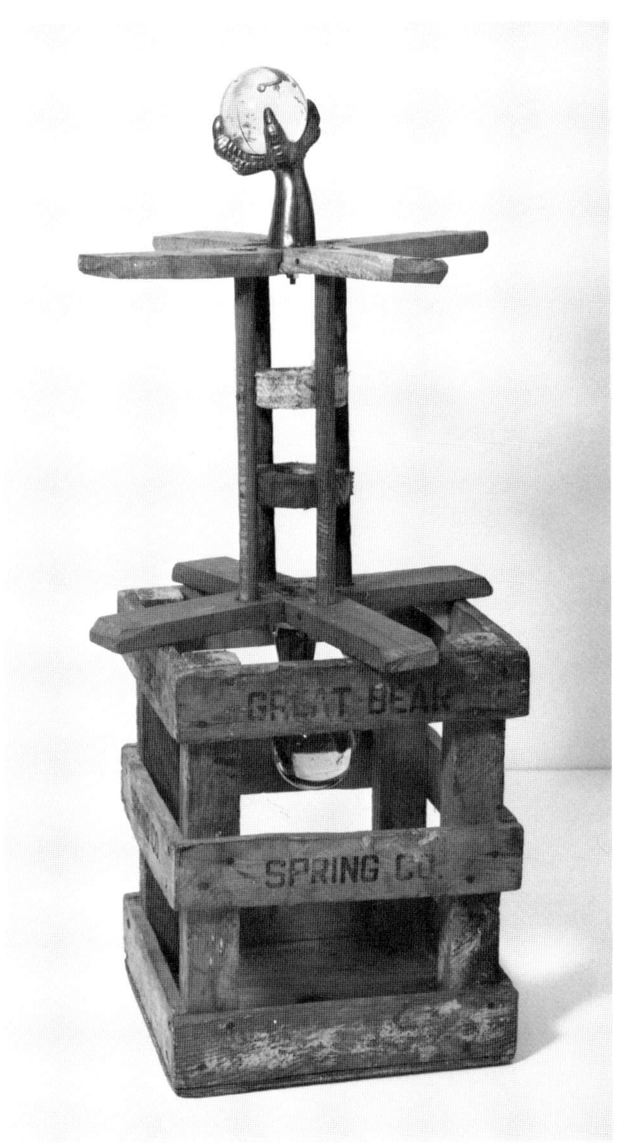

Ice Egg Metropole (Kabal American Zephyr) 1982
Construction
33¼ x 15 x 15″
Collection Roger I. Davidson, Toronto, Canada

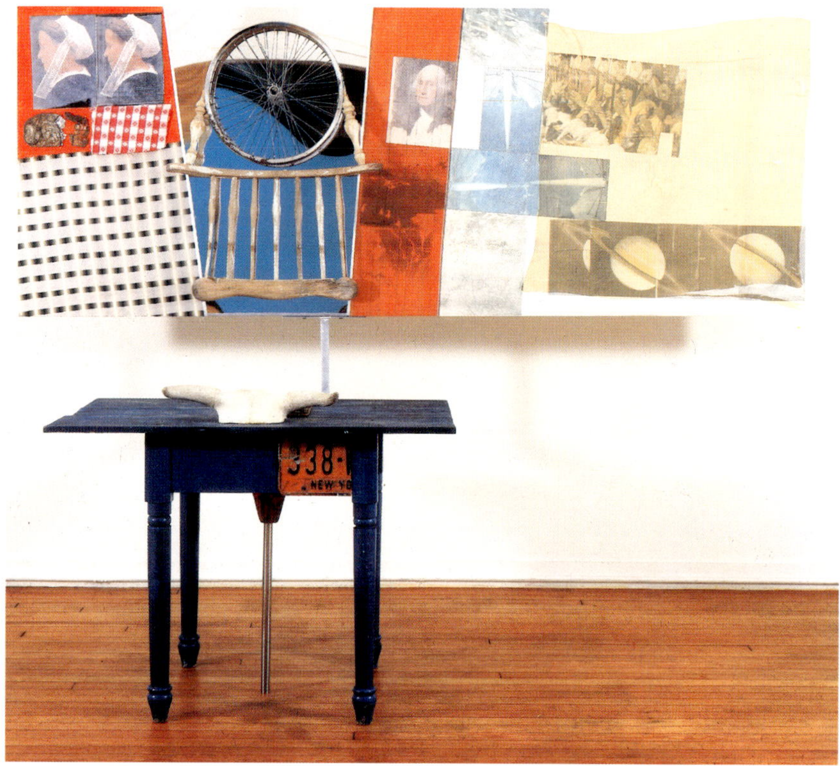

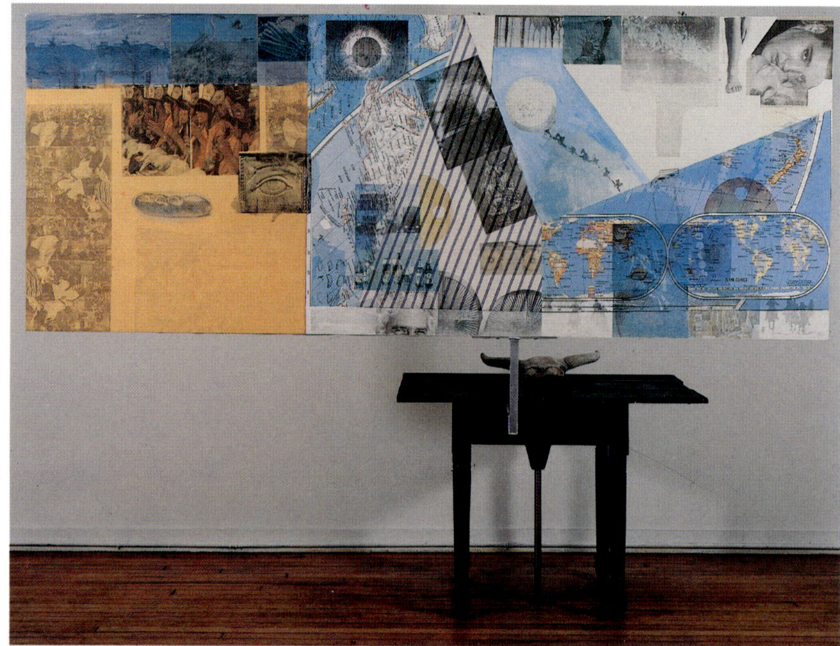

The Vain Convoy of Europe Out West (Kabal American Zephyr) 1982
(Two views)
Solvent transfer, acrylic and collage on wood veneer with objects
74 x 96½ x 41½"
Courtesy of the artist

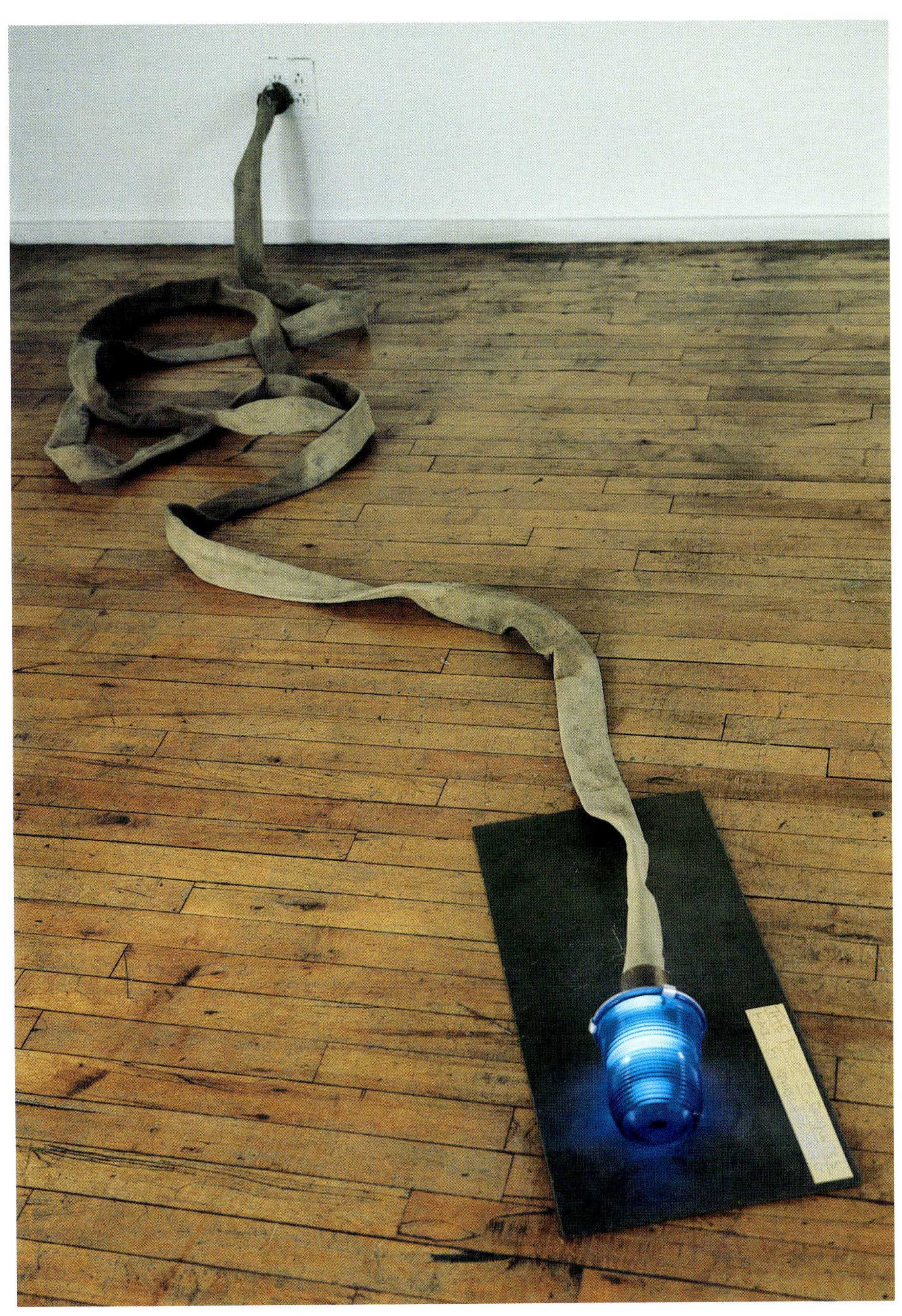

The Proof of Darkness (Kabal American Zephyr) 1981
Construction
Dimensions variable
Courtesy of the artist

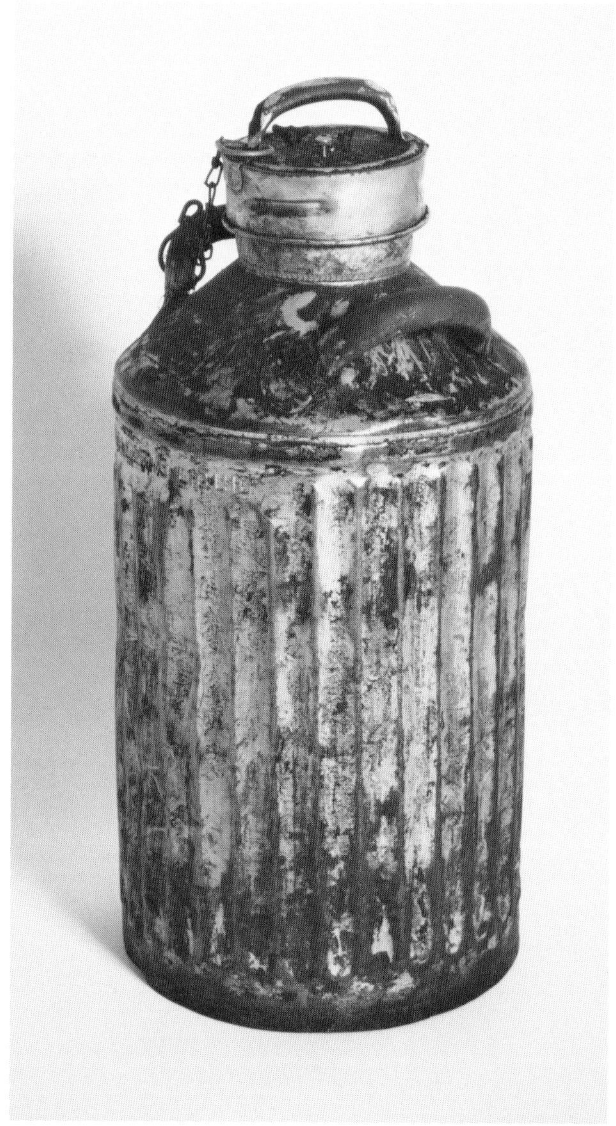

**Classic Cattleman Counter Column
(Late Kabal American Zephyr)** 1983
Construction
27 x 12½″ diam.
Courtesy of the artist

57

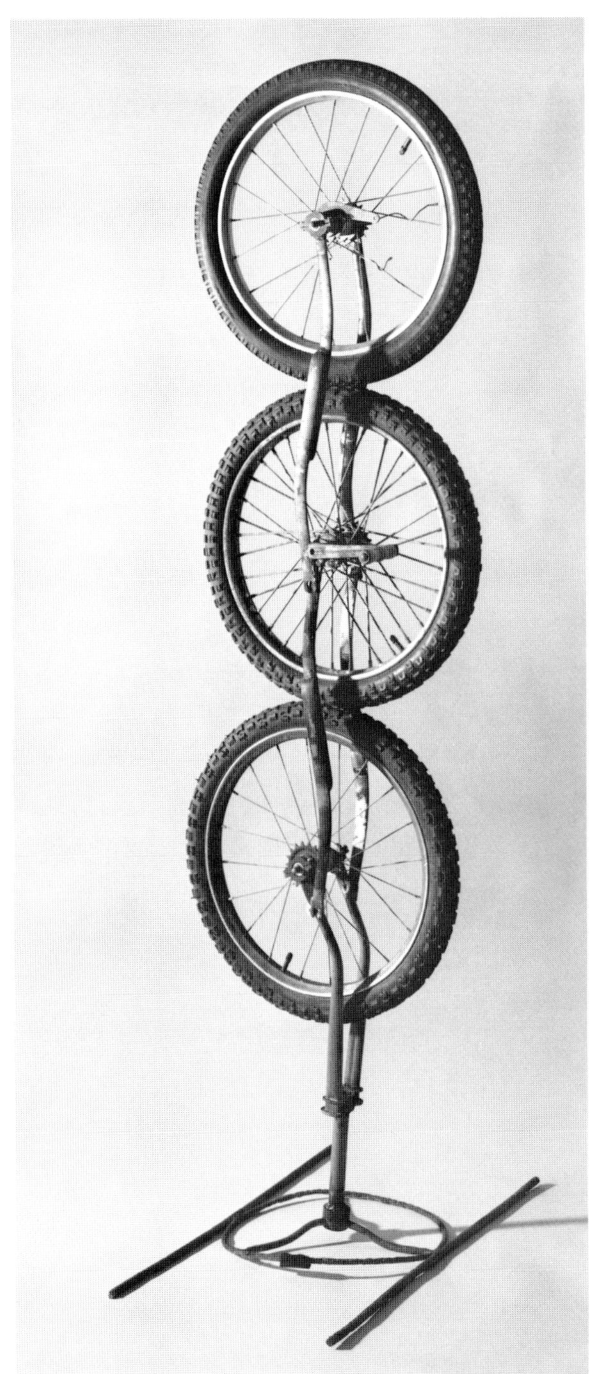

Untitled (Late Kabal American Zephyr) 1985
Construction
73½ x 24 x 28¼"
Courtesy of the artist

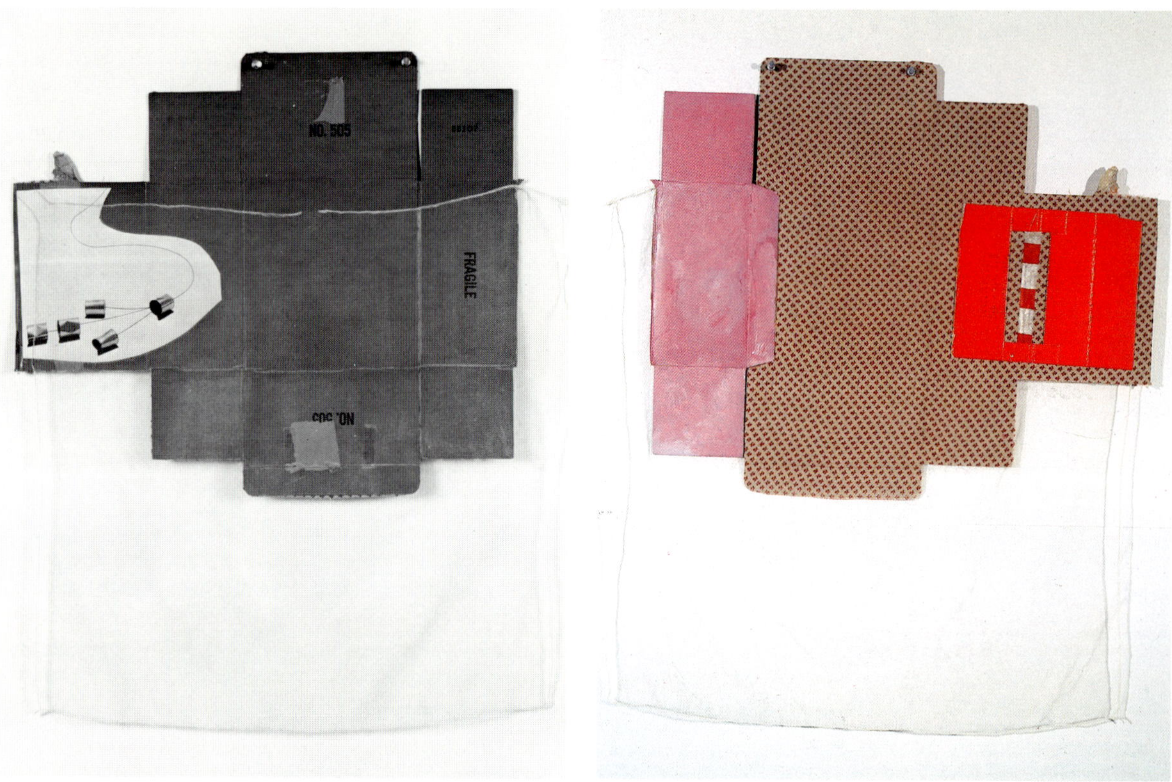

Lady Knight (Bifocal) 1982
(Double-faced)
Acrylic and collage on cardboard
29 x 24½″
Courtesy of the artist

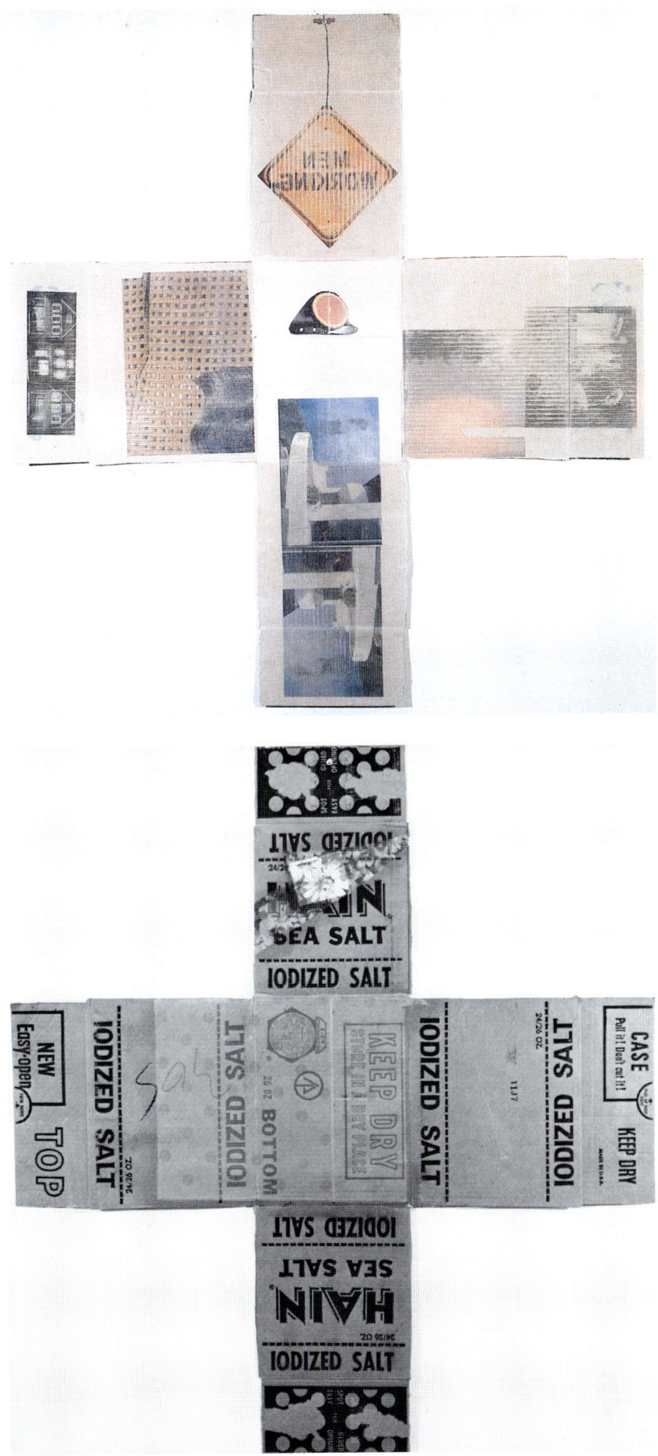

Land + Sea Cross (Bifocal) 1982
(Double-faced)
Solvent transfer, collage and pencil on cardboard
46 x 43″
Courtesy of the artist

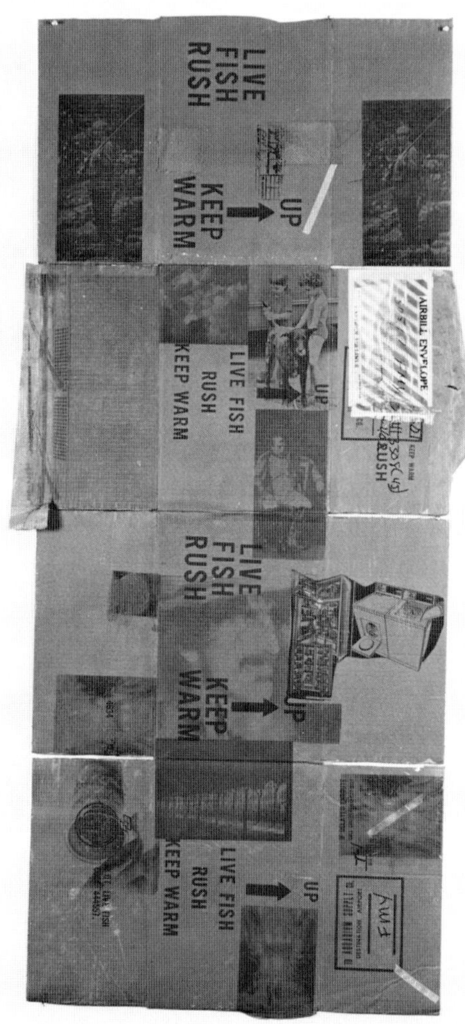

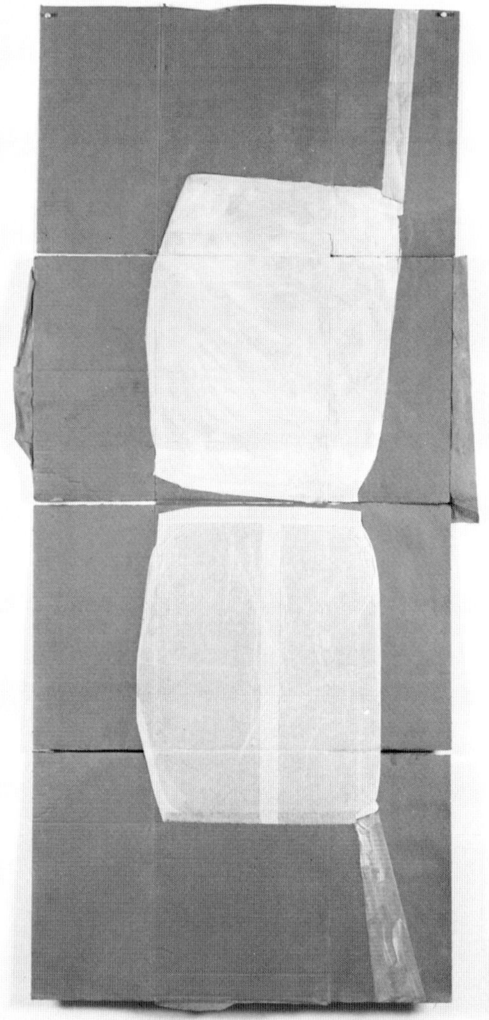

Live Fish Rush with Zappa (Bifocal) 1982
(Double-faced)
Solvent transfer, collage and acrylic on cardboard
68¼ x 33″
Collection Terry Van Brunt

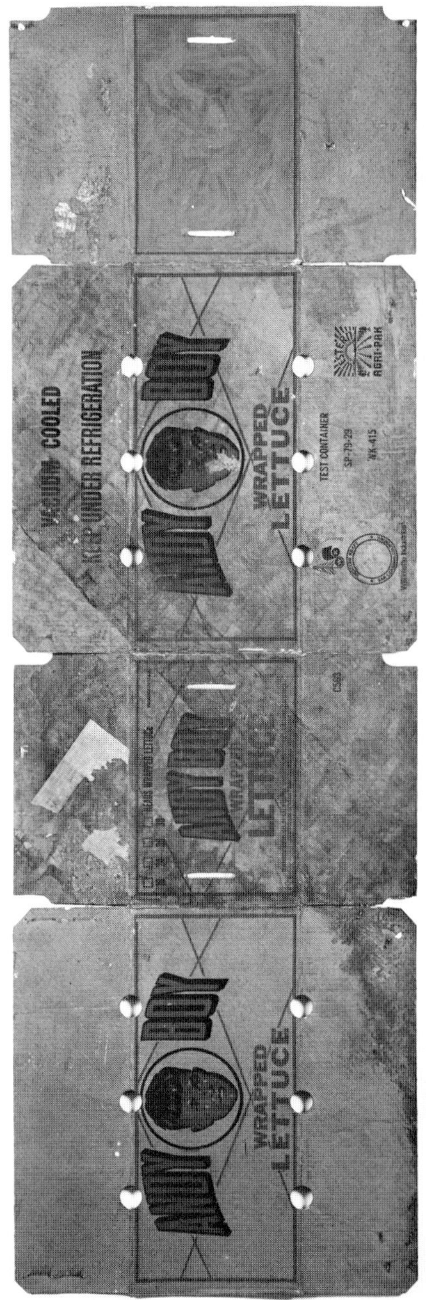
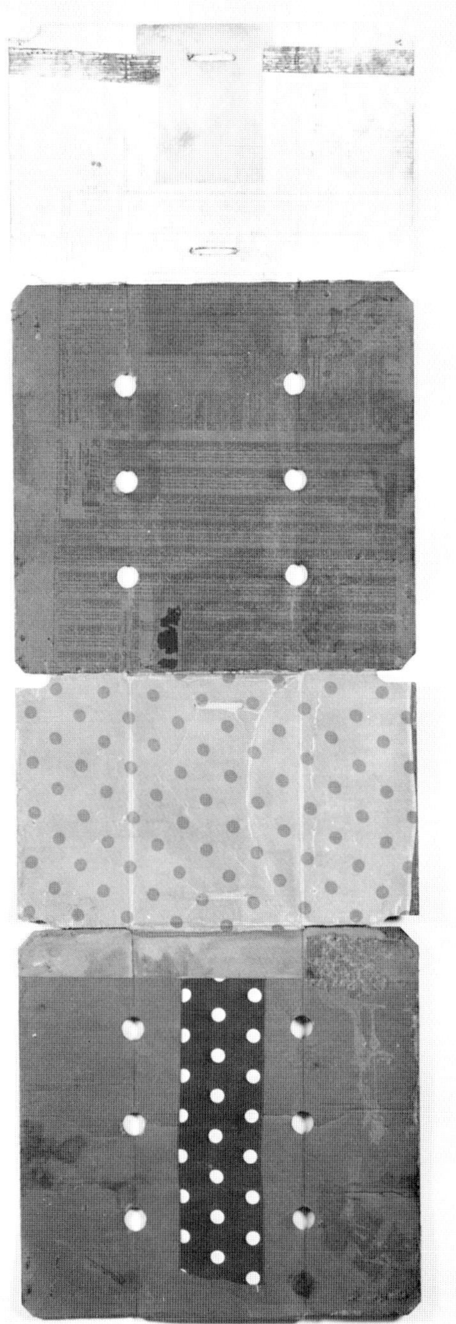

Andy Boy Polka (Bifocal) 1982
(Double-faced)
Solvent transfer, acrylic and collage on cardboard
77½ x 25¼″
Courtesy of the artist

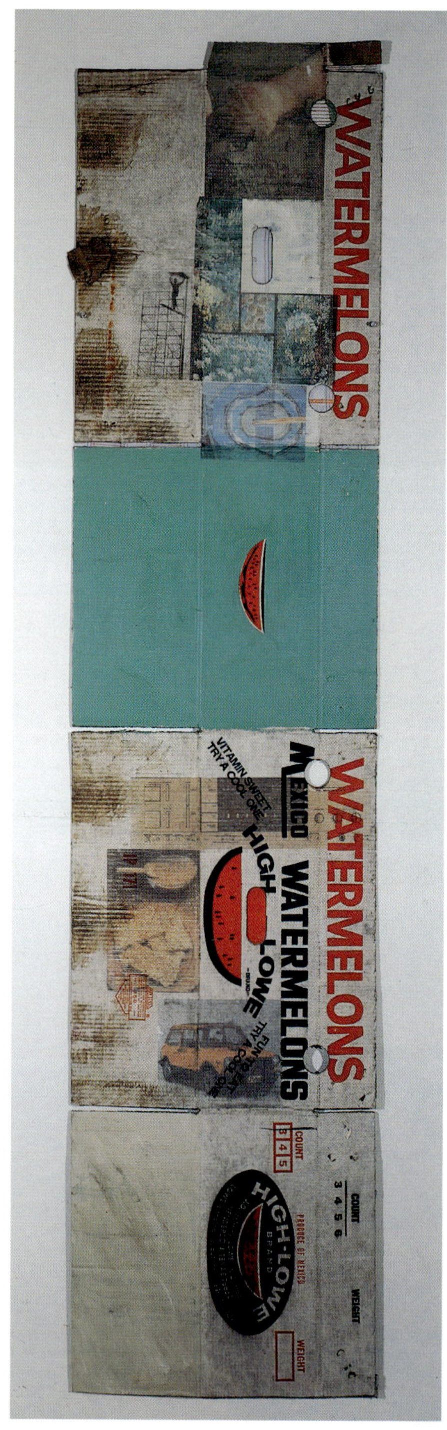

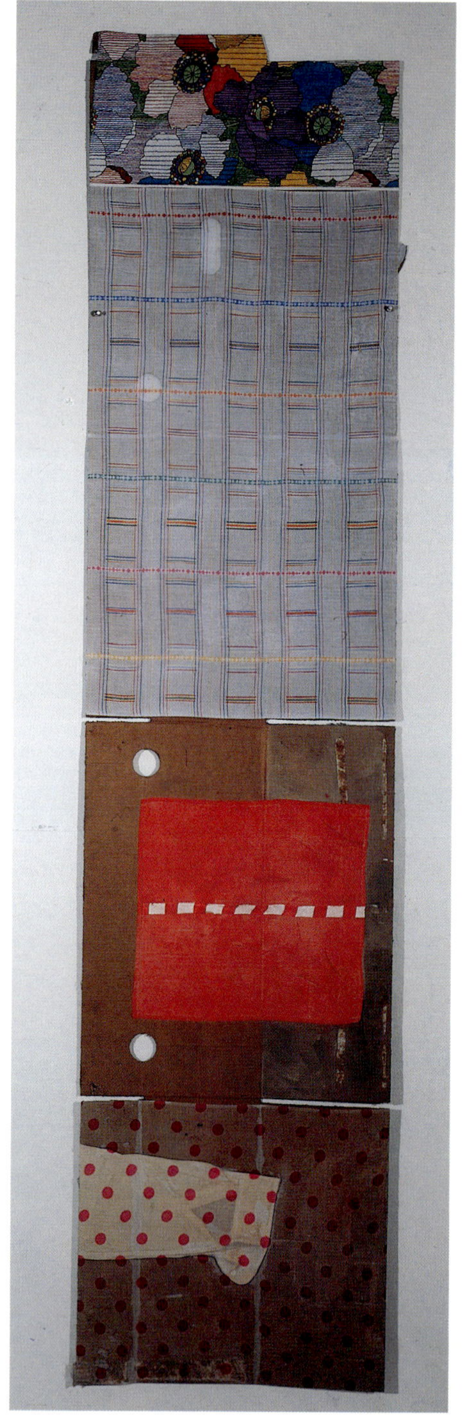

Watermelon Medley (Bifocal) 1982
(Double-faced)
Solvent transfer, acrylic, collage and pencil on cardboard
93½ x 22½″
Courtesy of the artist

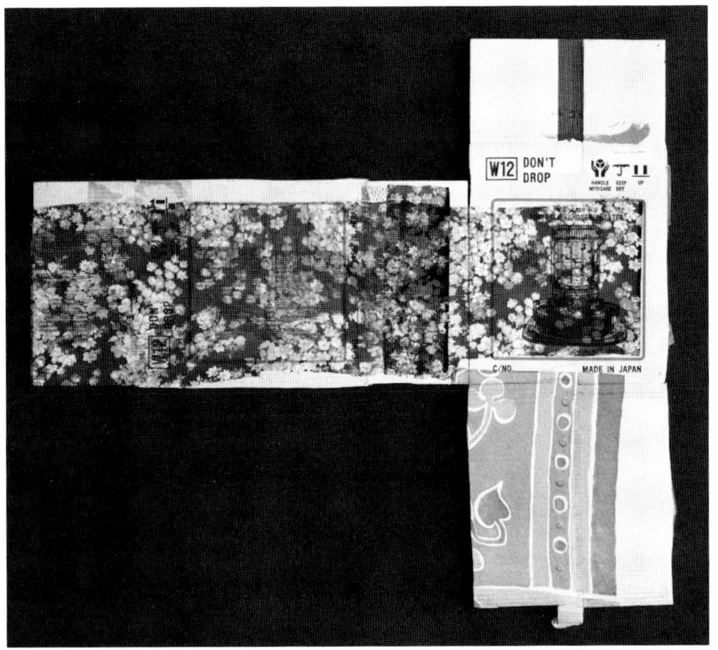

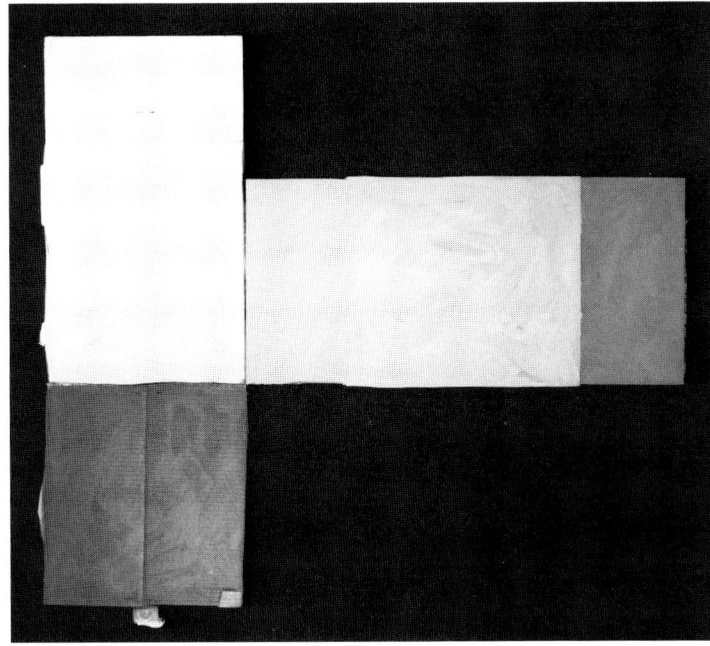

Garden Spot (Bifocal) 1982
(Double-faced)
Solvent transfer, acrylic and collage on cardboard
45 x 50½″
Collection Emil Fray

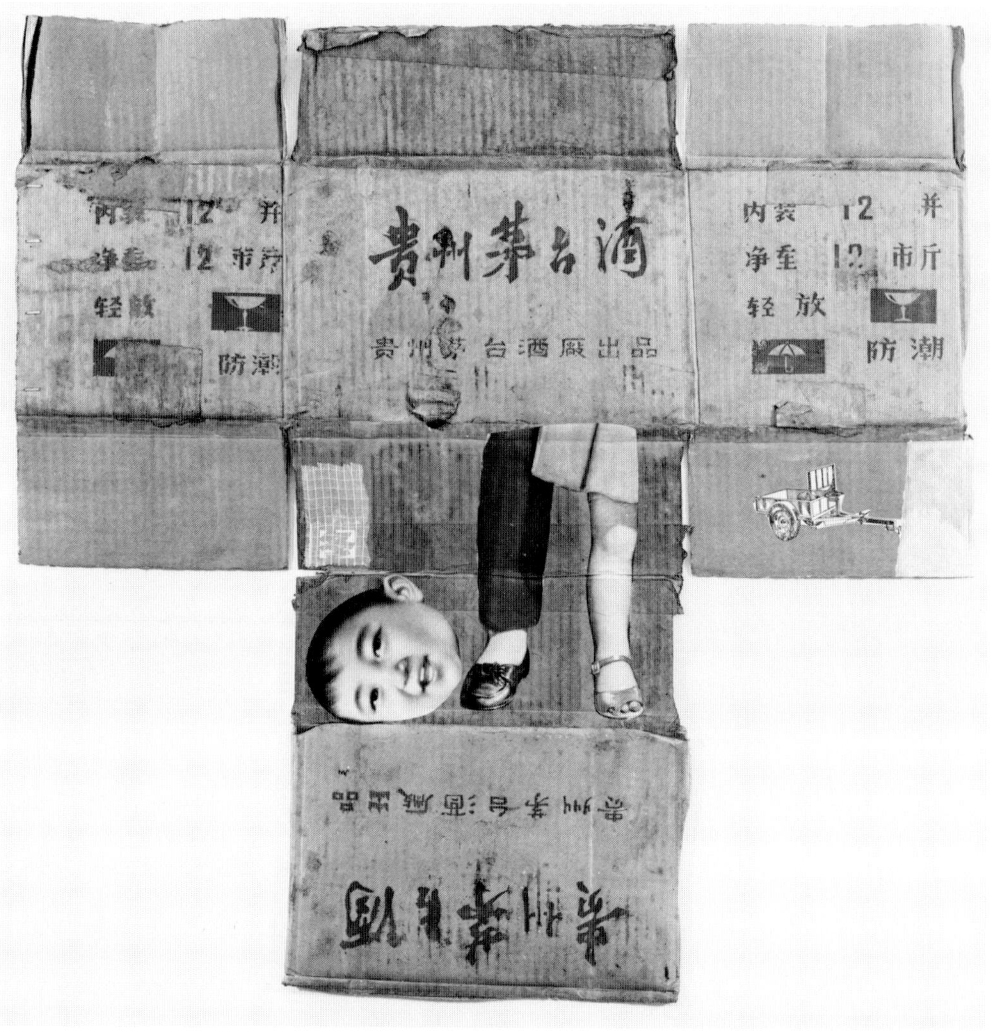

Paper Riddle 1982
Collage and acrylic on cardboard
32½ x 33″
Collection Terry Van Brunt

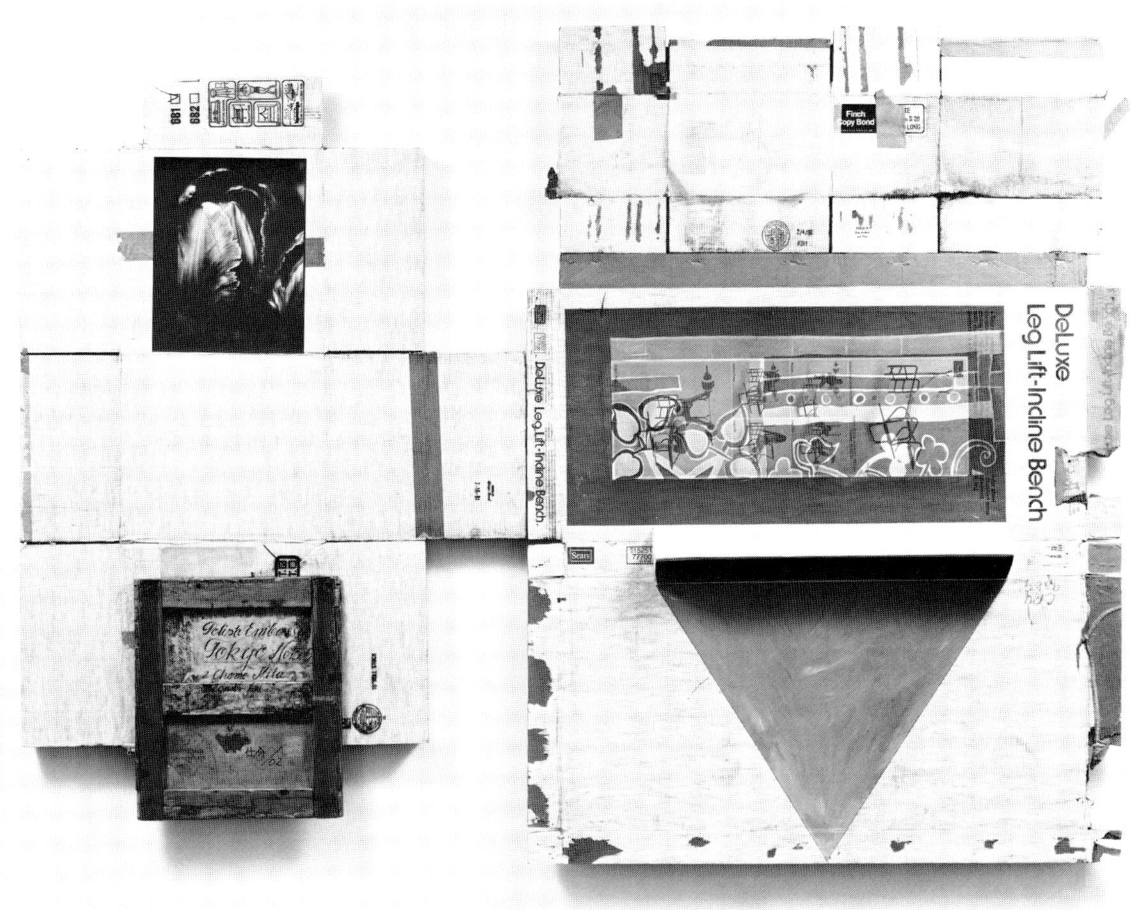

Parrot Buckboard 1982
Solvent transfer, pencil and collage on cardboard
85¼ x 117″
Courtesy of the artist

This documentation lists one-artist and group exhibitions from 1976 to the present which included unique works of art (not prints, multiples or photographs, for example). For exhibition listings prior to 1976, please refer to Robert Rauschenberg, Washington, D.C.: National Collection of Fine Arts, Smithsonian Institution, 1976.

1976

Galleria Civica d'Arte Moderna, Palazzo dei Diamanti, Ferrara, Italy. *Robert Rauschenberg*, Jan. 18–Mar. 7. Cat., texts by Paola Serra Zanetti, Daniel Abadie and David Bourdon.

Galerie H.M., Brussels. *Rauschenberg Hoarfrost*, Jan. 28–Mar. 10.

Leo Castelli Gallery, New York. *Rauschenberg Jammers*, Feb. 21–Mar. 13.

Russell, John. "Art: Alex Katz's Idyllic and Simplified World; Robert Rauschenberg." *The New York Times* (New York), Feb. 28, 1976, p. 22.

Hoesterey, Ingeborg. "New York." *Art International* (Lugano), vol. 20, no. 4–5, Apr.–May 1976, p. 69.

Andre, Michael. "New York Reviews: Robert Rauschenberg." *Art News* (New York), vol. 75, no. 5, May 1976, p. 121.

Grove, Nancy. "Arts reviews: Robert Rauschenberg." *Arts Magazine* (New York), vol. 50, no. 9, May 1976, p. 16.

Patton, Phil. "Reviews: Robert Rauschenberg." *Artforum* (New York), vol. 14, no. 9, May 1976, p. 62.

Sheffield, Margaret. "Review: New York: Exhibitions." *Studio International* (London), vol. 191, no. 981, May/June 1976, pp. 290–91.

The Greenberg Gallery, St. Louis, Missouri. Mar.

National Collection of Fine Arts, Smithsonian Institution, Washington, D.C. *Robert Rauschenberg*, Oct. 30–Jan. 2, 1977. Cat., texts by Joshua C. Taylor, Walter Hopps and Lawrence Alloway. Traveled to The Museum of Modern Art, New York, Mar. 25–May 17; San Francisco Museum of Modern Art, June 24–Aug. 21; Albright-Knox Art Gallery, Buffalo, New York, Sept. 23–Oct. 30; The Art Institute of Chicago, Dec. 3–Jan. 15, 1978.

Davis, Douglas. "Artist of Everything." *Newsweek* (New York), vol. 88, no. 17, Oct. 15, 1976, pp. 94–99.

Forgey, Benjamin. "An artist for all decades." *Art News* (New York), vol. 76, no. 1, Jan. 1977, pp. 35–36.

Gruen, John. "Robert Rauschenberg: An audience of one." *Art News* (New York), vol. 76, no. 2, Feb. 1977, pp. 44–48.

Perrone, Jeff. "Robert Rauschenberg." *Artforum* (New York), vol. 15, no. 6, Feb. 1977, pp. 24–31.

"La Vie des arts: Musées: New York: Rauschenberg sans passé." *L'Oeil* (Lausanne), no. 260, Mar. 1977, p. 47.

Russell, John. "Art That Sings." *The New York Times* (New York), Mar. 25, 1977, sec. 3, pp. 1, 19.

Stuckey, Charles F. "Reading Rauschenberg." *Art In America* (New York), vol. 65, no. 2, Mar.–Apr. 1977, pp. 74–84.

Tribiano, Calvin W. (Letter to the Editor), and Russell, John (Reply to Letter). "Letters: Art That Sings." *The New York Times* (New York), Apr. 8, 1977, sec. 3, p. 2.

"Rauschenberg: The World is a Painting." *Horizon* (New York), vol. 19, no. 3, May 1977, pp. 16–19.

"The Talk of the Town: Rauschenberg." *The New Yorker* (New York), vol. 53, no. 14, May 23, 1977, pp. 30–31.

Ratcliff, Carter. "New York." *Art International* (Lugano), vol. 121, no. 3, May–June 1977, pp. 60–61.

Busche, E. "Museum of Modern Art, New York; Ausstellung." *Kunstwerk* (Stuttgart), vol. 30, June 1977, pp. 49–50.

Bourdon, David. "A Critic's Diary: The New York Art Year." *Art In America* (New York), vol. 65, no. 4, July–Aug. 1977, p. 76.

Bremer, Nina. "Museen und Galerien: USA: New York." *Pantheon* (Munich), vol. 35, no. 3, July/Aug./Sept. 1977, pp. 274–75.

Shapiro, Lindsay Stamm. "New York/Sculpture." *Craft Horizons* (New York), vol. 37, no. 4, Aug. 1977, p. 65.

de la Falaise, Maxime. "Rauschenberg à Washington et à New York." *XXème Siècle* (Paris), vol. 39, no. 49, Dec. 1977, pp. 28–34.

Pieszak, D. "Robert Rauschenberg: from Port Arthur to Captiva." *New Art Examiner* (Chicago), vol. 5, no. 4, Jan. 1978, pp. 3, 23.

Forte Belvedere, Florence. *Hoarfrosts and Jammers*, Sept. 11–Oct. 10.

Alberta College of Art Gallery, Calgary, Canada. *Robert Rauschenberg—Glass Handle*, Oct. 12–Nov. 7. Cat.

Ace Gallery, Venice, California. *Jammers*. Traveled to Ace Gallery, Vancouver, Canada.

Galerie D, Brussels.

Galerie de Gestlo, Hamburg.

1977

Galerie Ileana Sonnabend, Paris. *Jammers*.
Crichton, Fenella. "Paris Letter: Rauschenberg." *Art International* (Lugano), vol. 21, no. 2, Mar.–Apr. 1977, pp. 57–58.

Leo Castelli Gallery, New York. *Spreads and Scales*, Apr. 23–May 23. Sonnabend Gallery, New York. *Spreads and Scales*, Apr. 23–May 14.
"Galerie Castelli und Ileana Sonnabend, New York: Ausstellung." *Kunstwerk* (Stuttgart), vol. 30, Aug. 1977, p. 67.

Rubinfien, Leo. "Reviews: New York: Robert Rauschenberg." *Artforum* (New York), vol. 52, no. 1, Sept. 1977, p. 33.

Zimmer, William. "Arts Reviews: Robert Rauschenberg." *Arts Magazine* (New York), vol. 52, no. 1, Sept. 1977, p. 33.

Linda Farris Gallery, Seattle. *Jammers and Hoarfrosts*, Sept. 5–30.

Janie C. Lee Gallery, Houston. *Hoarfrosts, Jammers, Spreads and Scales*, Oct. 29–Nov.

Ace Gallery, Venice, California. *New Paintings: Spreads and Scales*, Nov. 20–Dec. 14.

Galerie Rudolf Zwirner, Cologne.

1978

Galerie Ileana Sonnabend, Paris. May.

The Mayor Gallery, London. *Robert Rauschenberg: An Exhibition of Recent Work*, June 28–Aug. 11.
Vaizey, Marina. "Review." *Arts Review* (London), vol. 30, no. 13, July 7, 1978, p. 342.

Usherwood, Nicholas. "The Arts in Europe: Jasper Johns, Hayward Gallery, Robert Rauschenberg, Mayor Gallery." *Connoisseur* (London), vol. 198, no. 798, Aug. 1978, p. 336.

Vancouver Art Gallery, Canada. *Works From Captiva*, Sept. 8–Oct. 29.
Perry, Arthur. "Rauschenberg Meets Standard in Exhibition." *Artmagazine* (Toronto), vol. 11, no. 45, Sept./Oct. 1979, pp. 41–42. (Reprint from *The Province* [Vancouver], Sept. 1978).

Acquavella Contemporary, New York. Nov.–Dec.

Denise René/Hans Mayer, Dusseldorf. *Robert Rauschenberg*.
Friedrichs, H. "Galerie Denise René/Hans Mayer, Düsseldorf; Ausstellung." *Kunstwerk* (Stuttgart), vol. 33, no. 1, 1980, p. 68.

1979

Sonnabend Gallery, New York. *Two New Works by Robert Rauschenberg*, Jan. 13–Feb. 3.
Glueck, Grace. "Art: Puerto Rican Show in Bronx; Robert Rauschenberg (Sonnabend Gallery, 420 West Broadway)." *The New York Times* (New York), Jan. 26, 1977, sec. 3, p. 14.

Alloway, Lawrence. "Art." *The Nation* (New York), vol. 228, no. 5, Feb. 10, 1979, pp. 154–55.

Gibson, Eric. "New York Letter: Robert Rauschenberg." *Art International* (Lugano), vol. 23, no. 1, Apr. 1979, pp. 49–50.

Richard Gray Gallery, Chicago. *New Works*, Jan. 19–Mar. 10.

Galerie Mathilde, Amsterdam. Feb. 1–Mar. 3.

Akron Art Institute, Ohio. *Robert Rauschenberg: Spreads and Scales*, Feb. 3–Mar. 18.
Herr, Marcianne. "Robert Rauschenberg: Recent Works." *Dialogue* (Akron), vol. 1, no. 3, Jan.–Feb. 1979, p. 426.

Ace Gallery, Venice, California. *New Paintings*, Feb. 16–Mar. 24.

Richard Hines Gallery, Seattle. *Rauschenberg*, Feb. 19–Mar. 24.

Gloria Luria Gallery, Bay Harbor Islands, Florida. *Created in Florida*, Feb. 24–Mar. 19.
Edwards, Ellen. "Rauschenberg: He's 1 in the Art World." *The Miami Herald* (Miami), Feb. 25, 1979, pp. 1L, 10L.

Larson, Peter. "Rauschenberg: Captiva's New Old Master." *Island Reporter* (Captiva), Mar. 3, 1979, pp. 1–2.

Portland Center for the Visual Arts, Oregon. *New Works*, Apr. 2–30.

Kunsthalle Tubingen, West Germany. *Robert Rauschenberg— Das Zeichnerische Werk*, May 5–July 29. Cat., texts by Götz Adriani and Werner N. Greiner. Traveled to Kunstmuseum Hannover mit Sammlung Sprengel, West Germany, Aug. 19–Sept. 23.
Franzke, Andreas. "Museen und Galerien: Tubingen." *Pantheon* (Munich), vol. 37, no. 4, Oct./Nov./Dec. 1979, pp. 320–22.

"Journal: Deutschland: Wirklichkeit Als Collage: Wanderausstelung der Zeichnungen Robert Rauschenberg." *Du* (Zurich), Nov. 1979, p. 6.

The Center for Music, Drama and Art, Lake Placid, New York. *Hiccups*, June 28–July 15.

Musée de Toulon, France. *Rauschenberg*, July 14–Sept. 23. Cat., text by François Bazzoli.
    Blistene, Bernard. "Flash Art *France:* Rauschenberg." *Flash Art International* (Milan), no. 92–93, Oct.–Nov. 1979, p. 59.

Sonnabend Gallery, New York. *Slides*, Sept. 29–Oct. 20.
    Rickey, Carrie. "Reviews: New York." *Artforum* (New York), vol. 18, no. 4, Dec. 1979, p. 74.

Palm Springs Desert Museum, California. *Robert Rauschenberg*, Nov. 3–Dec. 2.

Art in Progress, Cologne.

1980

Gallery of Fine Art, Edison Community College, Fort Myers, Florida. *Robert Rauschenberg*, Feb. 3–27.
    "Rauschenberg Opens Exhibit." *Island Reporter* (Captiva), Feb. 1, 1980, p. B7.

    Shroder, Tom. "A Show to Put You on the Map." *Fort Myers News-Press* (Fort Myers), Feb. 7, 1980, p. D1.

    Bennett, Gale. "Art Review: Rauschenberg: A modern master." *Fort Myers News-Press* (Fort Myers), Feb. 8, 1980, pp. D1, D5.

    Faulkner, Mary. "Rauschenberg—Artist of the Eighties." *Lee Living* (Fort Myers), Mar. 1980, p. 45.

University Gallery of Fine Art, Ohio State University, Columbus. *Rauschenberg*, Feb. 14–Mar. 16.

Staatliche Kunsthalle, West Berlin. *Robert Rauschenberg: Werke 1950–1980*, Mar. 23–May 4. Cat., texts by Lawrence Alloway, Götz Adriani, Douglas M. Davis, William S. Lieberman and John Ciardi. Traveled to Kunsthalle, Dusseldorf, June 6–July 13; Louisiana Museum, Humlebaek, Denmark, Sept. 20–Nov. 23; Städtisches Kunstinstitut, Frankfurt, Dec. 4–Jan. 18, 1981; Städtische Galerie im Lenbachhaus, Munich, Feb. 4–Apr. 5; Tate Gallery, London, Apr. 29–June 14, 1981, as *Robert Rauschenberg: Retrospective*, cat., text by Alan Bowness.
    Meunier, L. "Rauschenberg in der Bundesrepublik." *Weltkunst* (Munich), vol. 50, no. 9, May 1, 1980, pp. 178–79.

    Blechen, Camilla. "Inmitten der Bilderflut." *Du* (Zurich), June 1980, p. 80.

    Kocks, Dirk. "Museen und Galerien: Düsseldorf." *Pantheon* (Munich), vol. 8, no. 4, Oct./Nov./Dec. 1980, pp. 316–17.

Muller-Mehlis, R. "Robert Rauschenberg." *Weltkunst* (Munich), vol. 51, no. 5, Mar. 1, 1981, pp. 532–35.

Burr, James. "Round The Galleries: The Gap Between." *Apollo Magazine* (London), vol. 113, no. 231, May 1981, p. 334.

Burn, G. "Tate Gallery, London: Exhibition Review." *Arts Review* (London), vol. 30, no. 10, May 22, 1981, p. 216.

Shone, Richard. "Current and Forthcoming Exhibitions: London." *The Burlington Magazine* (London), vol. 123, no. 940, July 1981, p. 436.

Lucie-Smith, Edward. "London Letter: Robert Rauschenberg." *Art International* (Lugano), vol. 24, no. 9–10, Aug.–Sept. 1981, pp. 70–71.

Shaw, John. "Robert Rauschenberg and the Profit Motif." *Antique Collector* (London), vol. 52, no. 11, Nov. 1981, p. 96.

Leo Castelli Gallery, New York. *Spreads and Scales*, Mar. 29–Apr. 19.

Ace Gallery, Venice, California. *Three of the Cloisters Series*, Apr. 24–Aug. 15.

Richard Hines Gallery, Seattle. May.

Anniston Museum of Natural History, Alabama. *Rauschenberg: A Retrospective of Lithographs, Paintings & Drawings from Castelli Graphics, New York*, June 6–Sept. 6. Traveled to Fay Gold Gallery, Atlanta, Jan. 9–Feb. 15, 1981.
    Hall, Randy. "Rauschenberg exhibit opens at museum June 6." *Anniston Star* (Anniston), May 10, 1980.

    "Famed Artist's Works To Be Shown Locally." *Oxford Sun* (Oxford, Ala.), May 28, 1980.

    Preble, Michael. "Reviews: Robert Rauschenberg: A Retrospective." *Atlanta Art Papers* (Atlanta), vol. 4, no. 5, Sept.–Oct. 1980.

    Weil, Debbie. "Retrospective Doesn't Offer Best Work of Rauschenberg." *The Atlanta Constitution* (Atlanta), Jan. 1981.

Ace Gallery, Venice, California. *Paintings*, Sept.

Cranbrook Academy of Art Museum, Bloomfield Hills, Michigan. *Robert Rauschenberg: Recent Work*, Sept. 14–Oct. 26.

Thomas Babeor Gallery, La Jolla, California. *Hoarfrosts, Bones and Publicons*, Oct. 1–30.

Baltimore Museum of Art, Maryland. *Robert Rauschenberg: 1970–1980*, Oct. 5–Nov. 30.

Ace Gallery, Vancouver, Canada. *Paintings*. Oct. 28–Nov. 30.

1981

The New Gallery of Contemporary Art, Cleveland. *Robert Rauschenberg: Recent Works: Spreads, Drawings, Etchings, Photographs*, Jan. 6–Feb. 21.

Gallery Gemini, Palm Beach, Florida. Jan. 13–20.

Galerie Watari, Tokyo, Jan. 16–Feb. 10.

The Sable-Castelli Gallery, Toronto, Canada. *Robert Rauschenberg*, Mar. 14–28.

Sonnabend Gallery, New York. *Rauschenberg at Sonnabend: Photems*, Mar. 28–Apr. 25.
> Westerbeck, Jr., Colin L. "Reviews: New York." *Artforum* (New York), vol. 19, no. 10, June 1981, pp. 92–93.
>
> Karmel, Pepe. "Review of Exhibitions: New York: Rauschenberg at Sonnabend." *Art In America* (New York), vol. 69, no. 8, Oct. 1981, pp. 139–40.

Institute of Contemporary Art, Boston. *Photems*. Sept. 15–Nov. 1.
> Allara, Pamela. "Boston: Robert Rauschenberg: Institute of Contemporary Art; Magnuson Lee; Jasper Johns: Thomas Segal." *Art News* (New York), vol. 81, no. 4, Apr. 1982, pp. 176–77.

The Mayor Gallery, London. *Robert Rauschenberg: Combine Drawings*, Oct. 12–Nov. 14.
> Burr, James. "Round the Galleries: The Classical Force of Pop." *Apollo Magazine* (London), vol. 114, no. 237, Nov. 1981, p. 346.
>
> Collier, Caroline. "Flash Art Reviews: London: Robert Rauschenberg." *Flash Art International* (London), no. 105, Dec. 1981–Jan. 1982, pp. 51–52.
>
> Francis, Richard. "Current and Forthcoming Exhibitions: London: Rauschenberg." *The Burlington Magazine* (London), vol. 124, no. 946, Jan. 1982, pp. 52–53.

1982

Gallery of Fine Art, Edison Community College, Fort Myers, Florida. *World Premiere of The 1st Footage of the ¼ mile or 2 Furlong Piece*, Feb. 6–26.
> Kotz, Mary Lynn. "Robert Rauschenberg's State of the Universe Message." *Art News* (New York), vol. 82, no. 2, Feb. 3, 1983, pp. 54–61.
>
> Faulkner, Mary. "A ¼ mile of design: Wrap yourself in Rauschenberg." *Fort Myers News-Press* (Fort Myers), Feb. 6, 1982.
>
> Zeiss, Betsy. "Around and About: Art Premiere an Experience." *The Breeze* (Cape Coral, Fla.), Feb. 9, 1982.

Flow Ace Gallery, Paris. *Sculpture by Robert Rauschenberg*, Oct. 23–Nov. 27.

Van Straaten Gallery, Chicago. *Rauschenberg: Paintings and Works on Paper*, Nov. 5–Dec. 10.

The Museum of Modern Art, New York. *Rauschenberg in China*, Dec. 2–Feb. 1, 1983.

Galleriet, Lund, Sweden.

1983

Sonnabend Gallery/112 and 136 Greene Street, New York. *Kabal American Zephyr Series*. Leo Castelli Gallery/142 Greene Street, New York. *Japanese Clayworks and Japanese Recreational Clayworks; 7 Characters; Chinese Summerhall*, Jan. 1–29. Cat., *7 Characters*, text by Donald Saff.
> Larson, Kay. "Rauschenberg's Renaissance: Three exhibitions show the artist at a New York peak." *New York* (New York), vol. 16, no. 1, Dec. 27, 1982–Jan. 3, 1983, pp. 50–56.
>
> Hughes, Robert. "The Arcadian as Utopian: Rauschenberg's rhapsodic energies fill four Manhattan shows." *Time* (New York), vol. 121, no. 1, Jan. 24, 1983, pp. 74–75.
>
> Smith, Roberta. "Clashes of Titans, Kisses of Death." *The Village Voice* (New York), Jan. 25, 1983, pp. 83, 85.
>
> Kuspit, Donald B. "Idolatry and Authority: notes from NYC." *Vanguard* (Toronto), vol. 12, no. 2, Mar. 1983, pp. 22–23.
>
> Bell, Jane. "New York Reviews: Robert Rauschenberg." *Art News* (New York), vol. 82, no. 4, Apr. 1983, p. 149.
>
> Marano, Lizbeth. "Review of Exhibitions: New York: Robert Rauschenberg at Castelli Greene St. and Sonnabend." *Art in America* (New York), vol. 71, no. 4, Apr. 1983, pp. 182–83.
>
> Silverthorne, Jeanne. "Reviews: New York: Robert Rauschenberg." *Artforum* (New York), vol. 21, no. 8, Apr. 1983, pp. 75–76.

Thomas Babeor Gallery, La Jolla, California. *China Collages*, Jan. 7–Feb. 12.

Flow Ace Gallery, Los Angeles. *Robert Rauschenberg: A Selection of Works From the Last Decade*, Mar. 16–Apr. 9.

Jingxian, Anhui Province, People's Republic of China. *Robert Rauschenberg: 7 Characters, Unique Collages*, June–July.

Gallery of Fine Art, Edison Community College, Fort Myers, Florida. *The Second Footage of the ¼ Mile or 2 Furlong Piece*, July 22–Sept. 9.
  Faulkner, Mary. "Best footage forward: Robert Rauschenberg reveals the second leg of his personal artistic race." *Fort Myers News-Press* (Fort Myers), July 22, 1983, pp. 10, 40.

  "Rauschenberg exhibit remains at EEC." *Islander* (Captiva-Sanibel, Fla.), Aug. 2, 1983.

  Faulkner, Mary, "Critic's Corner: Mixed reactions provide footage for artist Robert Rauschenberg." *Fort Myers News-Press* (Fort Myers), Aug. 14, 1983.

Prince Hotel, Tokyo. *Rauschenberg/Shigaraki*, Feb. 15.

K.B.S. Kaikan, Kyoto. *Rauschenberg/Shigaraki*, Feb. 21–26.

Galleria di Franca Mancini, Pesaro, Italy. *Rauschenberg/Performance, 1954–1983*, Aug. 11–Sept. 30. Cat., text by Nina Sundell. Traveled (expanded version) to Arthur A. Houghton, Jr., Gallery, The Cooper Union for the Advancement of Science and Art, New York, Dec. 7–22; Contemporary Arts Museum, Houston, May 12–June 24, 1984; Cleveland Center for Contemporary Art, Sept. 7–Oct. 8; North Carolina Museum of Art, Raleigh, Dec. 18–Feb. 17, 1985; Norton Gallery and School of Art, West Palm Beach, Florida, Mar. 9–Apr. 23; The University Art Museum, California State University, Long Beach, July 15–Sept. 15.
  "New York Day by Day: The Missing Chickens." *The New York Times* (New York), Dec. 8, 1983, sec. 2, p.3.

  Shepherd, Joan. "The Arts Community: Rauschenberg/Performance is artist's work for stage." *New York Daily News* (New York), Dec. 11, 1983.

  Sharp, Christopher. "Arts + People: Painting and Performance with the Father of Pop Art." *Women's Wear Daily* (New York), Dec. 14, 1983, p. 28.

  "An Opinionated Survey of the week's Events: *Rauschenberg/Performance*." *The Village Voice* (New York), Dec. 27, 1983.

  McEvilley, Thomas. "Reviews: New York: Robert Rauschenberg, Houghton Gallery, Cooper Union." *Artforum* (New York), vol. 22, no. 7, Mar. 1984, p. 82.

  Everingham, Carol J. "Rauschenberg performance colorful, eccentric." *The Houston Post* (Houston), May 17, 1984, p. 1E.

  Johnson, Patricia C. "Art: A moveable feast not so appetizing." *The Houston Chronicle* (Houston), May 20, 1984, "Zest" sec., pp. 17–18.

Mengel, Liz. "Robert Rauschenberg/Performance Contemporary Arts Museum Opening, May 15." *Public News* (Houston), issue 118, June 1, 1984, p. 6.

  Apple, Jackie. "Revisiting a Frontier." *Artweek* (Oakland), vol. 16, no. 29, Sept. 7, 1985, p. 5.

Maryland Institute, College of Art, Baltimore. *Images from China*, Oct. 12–Nov. 13.
  Dorsey, John. "Rauschenberg in China: collages, photographs." *The Sun* (Baltimore), Oct. 19, 1983, pp. B1, B4.

  Purchase, Steve. "Rauschenberg takes a photographic trek through China cities." *The Evening Sun* (Baltimore), Oct. 20, 1983, pp. 3, 15.

  Purchase, Steve. "Collages from China by Rauschenberg will delight the eye." *The Evening Sun* (Baltimore), Oct. 27, 1983, pp. 3, 10–11.

Marianne Friedland Gallery, Toronto, Canada. *Important Works by Robert Rauschenberg*, Oct. 22–Nov. 9.

Susanne Hilberry Gallery, Birmingham, Michigan. *Drawings*, Oct. 22–Nov. 29.

Australian National Gallery, Canberra. *Robert Rauschenberg*, Dec. 5–Jan. 31, 1984.

1984

Gallery of the Port Arthur Public Library, Texas. *Robert Rauschenberg Exhibition*, Feb. 4–19. Cat., text by Lynne Lokensgard.
  Roberson, Pam. "Rauschenberg exhibit reveals artist's success." *Port Arthur News* (Port Arthur), Feb. 5, 1984, pp. 1E–2E.

  Everingham, Carol J. "Return of Rauschenberg worth a celebration." *The Houston Post* (Houston), Feb. 8, 1984, p. 1E.

  Johnson, Patricia C. "Rauschenberg: 'I love working in different mediums (because) I don't want to get too sure of myself in any one'." *The Houston Chronicle* (Houston), Feb. 12, 1984, "Zest" sec., pp. 15, 43.

Galerie Beyeler, Basel, Switzerland. *Robert Rauschenberg*, Mar.–May. Cat., text by Götz Adriani.

Heland Thordén Wetterling Galleries, Stockholm. *Robert Rauschenberg*, Mar. 15–Apr. 23.

Center for the Fine Arts, Miami. *The 1st 400 feet or more than ½ a Furlong of the ¼ mile or 2 Furlong Piece*, May 5–July 1.
  Chandler, Mary. "When will this work end? He can't tell." *The Miami Herald* (Miami), May 5, 1984, "Living Today" sec., pp. 1C, 2C.

Fondation Maeght, St. Paul de Vence, France. *Robert Rauschenberg: Peintures récentes*, May 12–June 30. Cat., text by Nan Rosenthal.
  "En sortant de Rauschenberg prenez le Métro." *Connaissance des Arts* (Paris), no. 387, May 1984, p. 32.

Allen Street Gallery, Dallas. *Robert Rauschenberg: Photem Series 1*, Sept. 8–Oct. 14.

Gallery of Fine Art, Edison Community College, Fort Myers, Florida. *Robert Rauschenberg: Salvage Series.* Oct. 6–9. Faulkner, Mary. "Critic's Corner: Robert Rauschenberg's 4-day show proves again his mastery of color." *Fort Myers News-Press* (Fort Myers), Oct. 7, 1984.

Sonnabend Gallery, New York. *Robert Rauschenberg: New Works*, Oct. 20–Nov. 17.

1985

Fundación Juan March, Madrid. *Rauschenberg*, Feb.–Mar. Traveled to Fundació Joan Miró, Barcelona, Mar. 28–May 19.

John and Mable Ringling Museum of Art, Sarasota, Florida. *Robert Rauschenberg: Works from the Salvage Series*, Mar. 21–May 19. Cat., text by Mark Ormond.

Rauschenberg Overseas Culture Interchange (R.O.C.I.). Organized by Robert Rauschenberg. A five-year traveling exhibition, whose contents change at each venue with the addition of works made by the artist in collaboration with local artists and craftsmen. A catalogue, containing a statement by an internationally known writer or poet, is produced for each tour nation. Opened at Museo Rufino Tamayo, Mexico City, Mexico, Apr. 17–June 23, cat., text by Octavio Paz. Traveled to the Museo Nacional de Bellas Artes, Santiago, Chile, July 17–Aug. 18, cat., text by José Donoso; Museo de Arte Contemporaneo de Caracas, Venezuela, Sept. 12–Oct. 27; National Art Gallery, Beijing, People's Republic of China, Nov. 18–Dec. 5; Tibet, People's Republic of China, opened Dec. 2. Will travel worldwide through 1989, culminating at the National Gallery of Art, Washington, D.C.
McGill, Douglas C. "Art People: Rauschenberg's 'Rocky' Starting Next April." *The New York Times* (New York), Dec. 28, 1984, sec. 3, p. 32.

Moorman, Margaret. "Rocky Road to Peace and Understanding." *Art News* (New York), vol. 85, no. 2, Feb. 1985, p. 11.

Hackett, George. "Newsmakers." *Newsweek* (New York), vol. 105, no. 24, June 10, 1985, p. 61.

Gamarkian, Barbara. "Rauschenberg Carrying His Art to Many Lands." *The New York Times* (New York), Aug. 3, 1985, p. 13.

1976

New Gallery of Contemporary Art, Cleveland. *American Pop Art and the Culture of the Sixties*, Jan. 10–Feb. 21. Cat., texts by Nina Sundell and C. Nathanson.

Fendrick Gallery, Washington, D.C. *The Book as Art*, Jan. 12–Feb. 14. Cat., text by Daniel Fendrick.
Kernan, Michael. "Images in Words, Paintings and Paper." *Washington Post* (Washington, D.C.), Jan. 22, 1976, p. 15G.

Forgey, Benjamin. "Sculpture by the Book." *Washington Star* (Washington, D.C.), Feb. 8, 1976, p. 24G.

The Solomon R. Guggenheim Museum, New York. *Twentieth Century American Drawings: Three Avant-Garde Generations*, Jan. 23–Mar. 23. Cat., text by Diane Waldman. Traveled to Staatliche Kunsthalle, Baden-Baden, West Germany, May 27–July 11; Bremen Kunsthalle, West Germany, July 18–Aug. 29.
Smith, Roberta. "Drawing Now (and then)." *Artforum* (New York), vol. 14, no. 8, Apr. 1976, pp. 52–59.

The Museum of Modern Art, New York. *Drawing Now*, Jan. 23–Mar. 9. Cat., text by Bernice Rose. Traveled to Kunsthaus, Zurich, Oct. 10–Nov. 14; Staatliche Kunsthalle, Baden-Baden, West Germany, Nov. 25–Jan. 16, 1977; Albertina Museum, Vienna, Jan. 28–Mar. 6; Sonja Henie-Niels Onstad Foundations, Oslo, Mar. 17–Apr. 24; Tel Aviv Museum, Israel, May 12–July 2.
Russell, John. "Drawing Now, One of the Modern's Best." *The New York Times* (New York), Jan. 24, 1976, p. 23.

Fort Worth Art Museum, Texas. *The Great American Rodeo*, Jan. 25–Apr. 11. Cat., texts by Richard Koshalek and Jay Belloli. Traveled to Colorado Springs Fine Arts Center, Colorado, Aug. 1–29; Witte Memorial Museum, San Antonio, Feb. 5–Apr. 3, 1977.

Albright-Knox Art Gallery, Buffalo, New York. *Heritage and Horizon: American Painting 1776–1976*, Mar. 6–Apr. 11. Cat. Traveled to The Detroit Institute of Arts, May 5–June 13; The Toledo Museum of Art, Ohio, July 4–Aug. 15; The Cleveland Museum of Art, Sept. 8–Oct. 10.

The Art Institute of Chicago. *Seventy-second American Exhibition*, Mar. 13–May 9. Cat., texts by James A. Speyer and Anne Rorimer.

Whitney Museum of American Art, New York. *200 Years of American Sculpture*, Mar. 16–Sept. 26. Cat., texts by David Rockefeller, Tom Armstrong, Norman Feder, Wayne Craven, Daniel Robbins, Rosalind E. Krauss, Barbara Haskell and Marcia Tucker.

Galerie Beyeler, Basel, Switzerland. *Autres Dimensions: Collages, Assemblages, Reliefs*, June–Sept. Cat., text by Andreas Franzke.

The Museum of Modern Art, New York. *Hand Paper: Prints and Unique Works*, June 28–Sept. 22.

The Minneapolis Institute of Arts. *American Master Drawings and Watercolors*, Sept. 2–Oct. 24. Organized by the American Federation of Arts. Cat., text by Theodore E. Stebbins, Jr. Traveled to Whitney Museum of American Art, New York, Nov. 23–Jan 23, 1977; The California Palace of the Legion of Honor, San Francisco, Feb. 19–Apr. 17.
Kramer, Hilton. "Art: Drawing from the American Past." *The New York Times* (New York), Nov. 26, 1976, sec. 3, p. 20.

Canaday, John. "John Canaday on American Drawings at Whitney." *Art/World* (New York), vol. 1, no. 4, Dec. 11, 1976.

Glueck, Grace. "Art People." *The New York Times* (New York), Jan. 14, 1977, sec. 3, p. 17.

Kuh, Katharine. "Fine Arts: American Drawings: A Salute." *Saturday Review* (New York), vol. 4, no. 10, Mar. 5, 1977, pp. 43–45.

Galerie Beyeler, Basel, Switzerland. *America—America*, Oct.–Dec.

The Mayor Gallery, London. *USA*USA*, Nov. 10–Dec. 17.
Vaizey, Marina. "U.S.A., U.S.A." *Arts Review* (London), Nov. 28, 1976.

"USA—USA." *Art Monthly* (London), Dec./Jan. 1976–77.

Renwick Gallery of the National Collection of Fine Arts, Smithsonian Institution, Washington, D.C. *The Object as Poet*, Dec. 15–June 26, 1977. Cat., texts by Lloyd E. Herman and Rose Slivka. Traveled to The Museum of Contemporary Craft, New York, July 13–Sept. 25.
Hammel, Lisa. "A Show Where Literary Forms Imbue Crafts with Another Dimension." *The New York Times* (New York), Dec. 17, 1976, sec. 2, p. 2.

Conroy, Sarah Booth. "Poetic Objects: Bridging the Gap Between Art and Craft." *Washington Post* (Washington, D.C.), Dec. 26, 1976, sec. F, pp. 1, 3.

Gold, Barbara. "Poetry Can Be Fun in Renwick Show." *The Sun* (Baltimore), Jan. 9, 1977.

Slivka, Rose. "The Object as Poet." *Craft Horizons* (New York), vol. 37, no. 1, Feb. 1977, pp. 26–43, 63.

Hess, Thomas B. "For Each Man Kilns: The Thing He Loves." *New York* (New York), vol. 10, no. 31, Aug. 1, 1977, pp. 56–59.

Musée d'art moderne de la ville de Paris. *Boxes*, Dec.–Jan. 1977. Cat.

Genesis Gallery, New York.

Nationalgalerie, West Berlin. *New York in Europa*.

1977

New Orleans Museum of Art, Louisiana. *Five from Louisiana*, Jan. 28–Mar. 27. Cat., supplement to *The Times-Picayune*, Jan. 30, 1977, texts by William A. Fagaly, Tennessee Williams, Liza Bear, Philip Glass, Calvin Tomkins and Calvin Harlan.

Rose, Barbara. "The Bayou Bunch." *Vogue* (New York), vol. 167, no. 1, Jan. 1977, p. 40.

Glade, Luba. "NOMA's Extravaganza of the Avant Garde." *The States-Item Lagniappe* (New Orleans), Feb. 5–11, 1977, p. 8.

Jordan, George E. "'I Enjoyed It, but Is It Art?'" *The Times-Picayune* (New Orleans), Feb. 6, 1977, sec. 3, p. 4.

Flake, Carol. "NOMA's '5 Stylish Sons and Daughters of Louisiana'." *Figaro* (New Orleans), Feb. 9, 1977, p. 24.

Lippard, Lucy R. "Report from New Orleans: You Can Go Home Again: Five From Louisiana." *Art In America* (New York), vol. 65, no. 4, July–Aug. 1977, pp. 22–23, 25.

Glade, Luba B. "The Nation: New Orleans: 'Five from Louisiana'." *Art News* (New York), vol. 76, no. 6, Summer 1977, pp. 163–66.

Whitney Museum of American Art, New York. *Permanent Collection: 30 Years of American Art 1945–1975*, Jan. 29–Oct. 23.

Newport Art Museum, Rhode Island. *Two Decades of Exploration: Homage to Leo Castelli on the Occasion of His Twentieth Anniversary*, Feb. 13–Mar. 27.

Fendrick Gallery, Washington, D.C., *The Book as Art II*, Feb. 15–Mar. 12. Cat., text by Daniel Fendrick.

Institute of Contemporary Art, University of Pennsylvania, Philadelphia. *Improbable Furniture*, Mar. 10–Apr. 10. Cat., texts by Robert Pincus-Witten and Suzanne Delehanty. Traveled to La Jolla Museum of Contemporary Art, California, May 20–July 6.

John Berggruen Gallery, San Francisco. *American Paintings and Drawings*, Mar. 30–May 7.

Museum Boymans van Beuningen, Rotterdam, The Netherlands. *De Fiets*, April–June 12. Cat., texts by Titia M. Berlage, Ebbinge Wuben, Renilde Hammacher, E. Langui and J. van der Wolk.

"Expositions: Pays-Bas." *Gazette des Beaux Arts* (Paris), no. 1304, Sept. 1977, supp., p. 20.

Sidney Janis Gallery, New York. *Less is More*, Apr. 7–May 7.

Whitney Museum of American Art Downtown Branch, New York. *New York on Paper*, Apr. 7–May 22.

Sterling and Francis Clark Art Institute, Williamstown, Massachusetts. *The Dada/Surrealist Heritage*, May 3–June 12.

The Fitzwilliam Museum, Cambridge, England. *Jubilation, American Art During the Reign of Elizabeth II*, May 10–June 18. Cat., text by Michael Jaffé.

Kunsthaus, Zurich. *Malerei und Photographie im Dialog von 1840 bis Heute*, May 13–July 24.

Geelhaar, Christian. "Museen und Galerien: Zürich." *Pantheon* (Munich), vol. 35, no. 4, Oct./Nov./Dec. 1977, p. 372.

Thomas Segal Gallery, Boston. *Inaugural Show*, May 18–Aug. 8.

Musée National d'Art Moderne, Paris. *Paris—New York*, June 1–Sept. 19. Cat., edited by Pontus Hulten; texts on Rauschenberg by Alfred Pacquement.

Sonnabend Gallery, New York. *Group Show*. June. Tatransky, Valentin. "Group Show: Sonnabend." *Arts* (New York), vol. 52, no. 2, Oct. 1977, p. 32.

Leo Castelli Gallery, New York. *Recent Work*, June 15–Sept. 17.

Whitney Museum of American Art Downtown Branch, New York. *Pop Plus*, June 20–Aug. 1.

Whitney Museum of American Art, New York. *20th Century American Art from Friends' Collections*, July 27–Sept. 27.

The Hayden Gallery, Massachusetts Institute of Technology, Cambridge. *Paper Forms: Hand-Made Paper Projects*, Sept. 2–Oct. 5. Cat., texts by Kathy Halbreich.

Minnesota Museum of Art, St. Paul. *American Drawing 1927–1977*, Sept. 6–Oct. 29. Traveled to Henry Art Gallery, Seattle, Jan. 6–Feb. 6, 1978; The Santa Barbara Museum of Art, California, Apr. 11–May 14.

The Sable-Castelli Gallery, Ltd., Toronto, Canada. *Drawings*, Oct. 1–22.

New York State Museum, Albany. *New York: The State of Art*, Oct. 8–Nov. 28.

Jacksonville Art Museum, Florida. *The Florida Connection*, Oct. 20–Nov. 20. Cat., texts by William Chandler, Bruce Dempsey and Bruce Smathers.

Philadelphia College of Art, Pennsylvania. *Artists' Sets and Costumes*, Oct. 31–Dec. 17. Cat., texts by Janet Kardon and Don McDonah.

Joe and Emily Lowe Art Gallery, Syracuse University, New York. *Critics' Choice*, Nov. 13–Dec. 11. Traveled to Munson-Williams-Proctor Institute, Utica, New York. Jan. 3–30, 1978.

Andrew Crispo Gallery, New York. *Twelve Americans: Masters of Collage*, Nov. 17–Dec. 30. Cat., text by Gene Baro.

Conroy, W.T. "Columbian Collage: American Art of Assembly," *Arts* (New York), vol. 52, no. 4, Dec. 1977, pp. 86–87.

National Collection of Fine Arts, Smithsonian Institution, Washington, D.C. *New Ways With Paper*, Dec. 2– Feb. 20, 1978.

Madison Art Center, Wisconsin. *Works on Paper by Contemporary American Artists*, Dec. 4–Jan. 15, 1978.

Salles de la Fondation Nationale, Paris. *Biennale de Paris.*

1978

Margo Leavin Gallery, Los Angeles. *Three Generations: Studies in Collage*, Jan. 26–Mar. 4.

The Seibu Museum of Art, Tokyo. *Biennale de Paris '59–'73*, Mar. 3–29. Cat., texts by Takahiko Okada, Georges Boudaille, Kenjiro Okamoto, Makoto Ooka, Tadao Ogura, Yousuke Nakahara and Yoshiaki Tono.

Whitney Museum of American Art Downtown Branch, New York. *Art at Work: Recent Art From Corporate Collections*, Mar. 10–Apr. 11.

Stamford Museum, Connecticut. *The Eye of the Collector*, Mar. 20–May 21.

Ace Gallery, Vancouver, Canada. Apr. 16–30.

San Francisco Museum of Modern Art. *Aesthetics of Graffiti*, Apr. 28–July 2. Cat., texts by Rolando Castellon and Howard Pearlstein.

Margo Leavin Gallery, Los Angeles. *Works on Art*, May 24– June 24.

Wade Gallery, Washington, D.C. May 25–July 31.

Northpark National Bank, Dallas. *Leo Castelli Gallery at Northpark National Bank*, June 15–Aug. 15.

Leo Castelli Gallery, New York. *Summer Group Show*, July 5–Sept. 23.

The Museum of Modern Art, New York. *Artists and Writers*, July 10–Oct. 3.

Whitney Museum of American Art, New York. *Art About Art*, July 19–Sept. 24. Cat., texts by Leo Steinberg, Jean Lipman and Richard Marshall. Traveled to North Carolina Museum of Art, Raleigh, Oct. 15–Nov. 26; Frederick S. Wight Art Gallery, University of California, Los Angeles, Dec. 17–Feb. 11, 1979; Portland Art Museum, Oregon, Mar. 6–Apr. 15.

   Raynor, Vivien. "Art People." *The New York Times* (New York), July 14, 1978, sec. 3, p. 22.

   Kramer, Hilton. "Art: 'About Art,' Parodies, at Whitney." *The New York Times* (New York), July 21, 1978, sec. 3, p. 17.

   Alloway, Lawrence. "Art." *The Nation* (New York), vol. 227, no. 5, Aug. 19–26, 1978, p. 157–58.

Whitney Museum of American Art Downtown Branch, New York. *Collage: Selections From the Permanent Collection*, Aug. 14–Sept. 8.

Aarhus Kunst Museum, Denmark. *America*, Sept. 2–24. Cat., texts by Kristian Jakobsen and Reinhold Hohl.

The Neuberger Museum, State University of New York, Purchase. *The Sense of Self: From Self-Portrait to Autobiography*, Sept. 24–Nov. 26. Organized by Independent Curators Incorporated, New York. Cat., texts by Nina Sundell, Ira Licht and Richard King. Traveled to the New Gallery of Contemporary Art, Cleveland, Jan. 13–Feb. 3, 1979; University of North Dakota Art Gallery, Grand Forks, Feb. 13–Mar. 8; Alberta College of Art Gallery, Calgary, Nov. 21–Dec. 19; Tangeman Fine Art Gallery, University of Cincinnati, Feb. 11–Mar. 8, 1980; The Allen Memorial Art Museum, Oberlin College, Ohio, Apr. 1–May 4.

   Frank, Peter. "The Self and Others," *The Village Voice* (New York), Nov. 27, 1978.

Leo Castelli Gallery, New York. *Group Show*, Oct. 28– Nov. 18.

Art Center College of Design, Pasadena, California. *Berggruen at Art Center*, Nov. 5–30.

The Museum of Modern Art, New York. *Gold* (Winter Penthouse Exhibition), Nov. 20–Feb. 19, 1979.

Albright-Knox Art Gallery, Buffalo, New York. *American Painting of the 1970s*, Dec. 8–Jan. 14, 1979. Cat., text by Linda L. Cathcart. Traveled to Newport Harbor Art Museum, Newport Beach, California, Feb. 3–Mar. 18; The Oakland Museum, California, Apr. 10–May 20; Cincinnati Art Museum, July 6–Aug. 26; Art Museum of South Texas, Corpus Christi, Sept. 9–Oct. 21; Krannert Art Museum, University of Illinois, Champaign, Nov. 11–Jan. 2, 1980.

Marion Goodman Gallery, New York. *Objects!* Cat., text by Nicolas and E. Calas, reprinted in *XXème Siècle* (Paris), no. 50, June 1978, p. 157.

1979

The Solomon R. Guggenheim Museum, New York. *Art in America after World War II*, Jan. 18–Feb. 25.

Hampshire College Art Gallery, Amherst, Massachusetts. *Images of the Self*, Feb. 19–Mar. 14. Cat., texts by Sally Yard and Irving Sandler.

Corcoran Gallery of Art, Washington, D.C. *The 36th Biennial Exhibition of Contemporary American Painting*, Feb. 24– Apr. 8. Cat., text by Jane Livingston.

   Forgey, Benjamin. "At the Corcoran Gallery, A Small But Stunning Biennial Presents the Work of Five Top American Painters." *Smithsonian* (Washington, D.C.), vol. 9, no. 2, 1979, pp. 80–87.

Lewis, JoAnn. "'Setting Standards,' at the Corcoran." *Art News* (New York), vol. 78, no. 4, Apr. 1979, pp. 85, 88–89.

Tannous, David. "Report from Washington: Big-Name Biennial, Plus…" *Art in America* (New York), vol. 67, no. 4, July–Aug. 1979, pp. 24–25.

Wright, Martha McWilliams. "Washington Letter." *Art International* (Lugano), vol. 23, no. 5–6, Sept. 1979, pp. 76–77.

Castelli Graphics, New York. *Drawings by Castelli Artists*, Mar. 3–24.

Whitney Museum of American Art Downtown Branch, New York. *Auto-Icons*, Apr. 18–May 23.

Everson Museum of Art of Syracuse and Onondaga County, New York. *A Century of Ceramics in the United States 1878–1978*, May 5–Sept. 23. Cat., text by Garth Clark. Traveled to Renwick Gallery of the National Collection of Fine Arts, Smithsonian Institution, Washington, D.C., Nov. 9–Jan. 27, 1980; Cooper-Hewitt Museum, The Smithsonian Institution's National Museum of Design, New York, Feb. 26–May 25; Flint Institute of Art, Michigan, June 15–Aug. 31; The De Cordova Museum, Lincoln, Massachusetts, Sept. 28–Nov. 23; The Philbrook Art Center, Tulsa, Dec. 15–Jan. 25, 1981; The Chicago Public Library Cultural Center, Feb. 23–Apr. 12; Allentown Art Museum, Pennsylvania, May 3–July 26; The Toledo Museum of Art, Ohio, Sept. 13–Oct. 18.

Nordstrom, Sherry Chayat. "Exhibit shows Americans 'Play with Fire and Clay'." *The Syracuse Post Standard* (Syracuse), June 1, 1979.

"A Hundred Years of Pottery." *The Christian Science Monitor* (Boston), July 18, 1979, p. 15.

Tipton, Barbara. "A Century of Ceramics in the United States." *Ceramics Monthly* (Columbus), vol. 27, no. 8, Oct. 1979, pp. 49–50.

Rosa Esman Gallery, New York. *Summer Summary*, June 5–July.

Williams College Museum of Art, Williamstown, Massachusetts. *Documents, Drawings and Collages: 50 American Works on Paper from the Collection of Mr. and Mrs. Stephen D. Paine*, June 8–July 5. Cat., texts by Stephen D. Paine, Franklin W. Kelly, Stephen Eisenman and Hiram C. Butler. Traveled to The Toledo Museum of Art, Ohio, Oct. 6–Nov. 18; John and Mable Ringling Museum of Art, Sarasota, Florida, Dec. 6–Mar. 1, 1980; The Fogg Art Museum, Harvard University, Cambridge, Massachusetts, Apr. 10–May 15.

Daniel Templon, Paris. *Une Peinture Américaine*, June 9–July 12.

Leo Castelli Gallery, New York. *Summer Group Show*, June 23–Sept. 15.

Aspen Center for the Visual Arts, Colorado. *American Portraits of the Sixties and Seventies*, June–Aug. Cat., texts by Philip Yenawine and Julie Augur.

The Metropolitan Museum of Art, New York. *Summer Loans*, July 17–Sept. 30.

La Jolla Museum of Contemporary Art, California. *Selections/Permanent Collection*, July 18–Aug. 19.

Sonnabend Gallery, New York. *Group Show*, Summer.

John Michael Kohler Arts Center, Sheboygan, Wisconsin. *Glass/Backwards*, Sept. 9–Oct. 28.

Institute for Art and Urban Resources, P.S. 1, Long Island City, New York. *Sound at P.S. 1*, Sept. 30–Nov. 18.

Centre Nationale d'Art et de Culture Georges Pompidou, Paris. *Autour Merce Cunningham*. Oct. 10–Nov. 12.

University Art Gallery, Wright State University, Dayton, Ohio. *Generative Issues: A Common Ground*, Oct. 30–Nov. 21.

Galerie d'Art Contemporain des Musées de Nice, France. *American Pop Art*, Nov. 9–Jan. 6, 1980.

Denver Art Museum, Colorado. *Poets and Painters*, Nov. 21–Jan. 13, 1980. Traveled to William Rockhill Nelson Gallery and Atkins Museum of Fine Arts, Kansas City, Missouri, Aug. 15–Sept. 28; La Jolla Museum of Contemporary Art, California, Oct. 17–Dec. 1.

San Antonio Museum of Art, Texas. *Twentieth-Century Drawings from the Whitney Museum of American Art*, Nov. 26–Jan. 14, 1980. Organized by the Whitney Museum of American Art, New York. Cat., text by Paul Cummings. Traveled to University of Iowa Museum of Art, Iowa City, Feb. 8–Mar. 23; Frederick S. Wight Art Gallery, University of California, Los Angeles, Apr. 6–May 4; Minnesota Museum of Art, St. Paul, June 18–July 25; J.B. Speed Art Museum, Louisville, Kentucky, Oct. 6–Nov. 17; Loch Haven Art Center, Orlando, Florida, Jan. 3–Feb. 15, 1981.

Hicks, Mary. *Artweek* (Oakland), Apr. 26, 1980, p. 5.

United States International Communications Agency, Washington, D.C. *The Artist at Work in America*, Winter 1979–1980. Traveled to Bulgaria.

1980

Fine Arts Gallery, University of South Florida, Tampa. *Five in Florida*, Jan. 7–Feb. 8. Cat., texts by Margaret Miller and Gene Baro.

Leo Castelli Gallery/142 Greene Street, New York. *Leo Castelli: A New Space*, Feb. 19–Mar.

Erlich, Robbie. "Group Show." *Arts* (New York), vol. 54, no. 10, June 1980, p. 43.

Joe and Emily Lowe Art Gallery, Syracuse University, New York. *Recent Acquisitions*, Feb. 10–Apr. 16.

Walker Art Center, Minneapolis. *Echoes of Picasso*, Feb. 10–Mar. 30.

Hampshire College Art Gallery, Amherst, Massachusetts. *A Sense of Place: The American Landscape in Recent Art*, Feb. 11–26. Cat., text by Sally Yard.

Visual Arts Museum, School of Visual Arts, New York. *The Object Transformed: Contemporary American Drawing*, Feb. 11–29.

North Carolina Museum of Art, Raleigh. *Collage*, Feb. 17–Mar. 16.

Allen Memorial Art Museum, Oberlin College, Ohio. *From Reinhardt to Christo*, Feb. 20–Mar. 19.

Galerie Beyeler, Basel, Switzerland. *Lettres et Chiffres*, Mar.–May.

Neuberger Museum, State University of New York, Purchase. *Hidden Desires*, Mar. 9–June 15.

Grand Palais, Paris. *91ème Exposition Société des Artistes Indépendants*, Mar. 13–Apr. 13.

Pace Gallery, New York. *Major Paintings and Reliefs of the 60's from a New York Private Collection*, Mar. 28–Apr. 26.

Montgomery Museum of Fine Arts, Alabama. *American Painting of the Sixties and Seventies: The Real/The Ideal/The Fantastic: Selections from the Whitney Museum of American Art*, Apr. 4–May 25. Cat., text by Mitchell D. Kahan. Traveled to Joslyn Art Museum, Omaha, Nebraska, July 25–Sept. 14; Museum of Fine Arts of St. Petersburg, Florida, Sept. 28–Nov. 9; Columbus Museum of Art, Ohio, Dec. 8–Jan. 15, 1981; Colorado Springs Fine Arts Center, Colorado, Feb. 1–Mar. 21; Sierra Nevada Museum of Art, Reno, Nevada, Apr. 11–May 23.

Amelie A. Wallace Gallery, State University of New York, College at Old Westbury. *Fabric into Art*, Apr. 14–May 9. Cat., text by Harriet Senie. Traveled to State Universities of New York at Alfred, Brockport and Albany.
Shirey, David L. "Originality in Fabric." *The New York Times* (New York), Apr. 27, 1980, Westchester County sec., p. 11.

Margo Leavin Gallery, Los Angeles. *Drawings*, May.

Lowe Art Museum, University of Miami, Coral Gables. *Fabrications*, May 1–Aug. 10. Traveled to Fine Arts Gallery, University of South Florida, Tampa, Sept. 15–Oct. 23.

Seagram Building, New York. *Self-Portraits*, May 19–Aug. 8.

Hirshhorn Museum and Sculpture Garden, Smithsonian Institution, Washington, D.C. *The Fifties: Aspects of Painting in New York*, May 22–Sept. 21. Cat., text by Phyllis Rosenzweig.
Smith, Roberta. "Report from Washington: The '50s Revisited, Not Revised." *Art in America* (New York), vol. 68, no. 9, Nov. 1980, pp. 47–51.

Whitney Museum of American Art, New York. *50th Anniversary Gifts and Promised Gifts*, June 3–Aug. 31.

Sonnabend Gallery, New York. *Group Show*, June 21–July 19.

Van Straaten Gallery, Chicago. *Group Show*, July 11–Aug. 31.

La Jolla Museum of Contemporary Art, California. *The Permanent Collection*, July 12–Aug. 31.

Kunsthaus, Zurich. *Reliefs*, Aug. 22–Nov. 2.

The National Gallery of Art, Washington, D.C. *The Morton G. Neumann Family Collection*, Aug. 31–Jan. 11, 1981. Cat., texts by E. A. Carmean, Jr., Sam Hunter, Trinket Clark and Elizabeth C. Rathbone. Traveled to The Art Institute of Chicago, Feb. 21–Apr. 19, 1981.

Cranbrook Academy of Art Museum, Bloomfield Hills, Michigan. *The Changing Canvas*, Sept. 14–Oct. 26.

Mary and Leigh Block Gallery, Northwestern University, Evanston, Illinois. *Collaborations: An Exhibition to Celebrate the Dedication of the Mary and Leigh Block Gallery and the Completion of the Fine and Performing Arts Center at Northwestern University*, Sept. 27–Oct. 6. Cat., text by Kathy K. Foley.

Grand Palais, Paris. *Foire Internationale d'Art Contemporain*, Oct. 23–29.

The Brooklyn Museum, New York. *American Drawing in Black and White*, Nov. 22–Jan. 18, 1981.

Castelli Graphics, New York. *Amalgam*, Nov. 22–Dec. 20.

Leo Castelli Gallery, New York. *Drawings to Benefit the Foundation for Contemporary Performance Art, Inc.*, Nov. 22–Jan. 18, 1981.

La Jolla Museum of Contemporary Art, California. *The Permanent Collection*, Dec. 6–Jan. 18, 1981.

Museum of the Palace of Fine Arts, Mexico City, Mexico. *Paintings in the U.S. from Public Collections in Washington, D.C.*

1981

Richard Hines Gallery, Seattle. *Group Exhibition: Major Works*, Jan. 9–Feb. 21.

Galleriet, Lund, Sweden. *Group Show*, Jan. 17–Feb. 4.

Neil G. Ovsey Gallery, Los Angeles. *Selections from Castelli: Drawings and Works on Paper*, Jan. 18–Feb. 21.

Jeffrey Fuller Fine Art at the Kron Art Gallery, Philadelphia. *Photography Influences Painting,* Feb. 1–Mar. 7.

John and Mable Ringling Museum of Art, Sarasota, Florida. *International Florida Artists,* Feb. 26–Apr. 26.

Gloria Luria Gallery, Bay Harbor Islands, Florida. *Leo Castelli Selects Johns, Judd, Lichtenstein, Rauschenberg, Rosenquist, Stella,* Feb. 27–Mar. 17.

The Mayor Gallery, London. *Major Paintings and Sculptures,* Mar. 2–30.
Watson, Francis. "Mixed Moderns." *Arts Review* (London), Mar. 13, 1981.
Mullaly, Terence. "Art: Hallowed modern names." *The Daily Telegraph* (London), Mar. 18, 1981.

The Museum of Modern Art, New York. *Recent Acquisitions: Drawings,* Mar. 19–June 2.

National Gallery of Art, Washington, D.C. *Contemporary American Prints and Drawings 1940–1980,* March 22–July 19. Cat., text by Andrew Robinson.

The Aldrich Museum of Contemporary Art, Ridgefield, Connecticut. *New Dimensions in Drawing,* May 2–Sept. 6. Cat., texts by Dorothy Mayhall and Richard E. Anderson.

University of Colorado Art Galleries, Boulder. *Mapped Art: Charts, Routes, Regions,* May 2–June 7. Organized by Independent Curators Incorporated, New York. Cat., text by Peter Frank. Traveled to The First Street Forum, St. Louis, Oct. 3–Nov. 15; The Arkansas Art Center, Little Rock, June 18, 1982–July 18; The Archer M. Huntington Art Gallery, The University of Texas at Austin, Aug. 1–Nov. 1; The Toledo Museum of Art, Ohio, Nov. 13–Jan. 2, 1983.

American Academy of Arts and Sciences, Cambridge, Massachusetts. *Bicentennial Exhibition,* May 15–16.

Leo Castelli Gallery, New York. *Benefit Exhibition for the Trisha Brown Dance Co.,* May 16–30.

Cologne. *Internationale Ausstellung Köln,* May 30–Aug. 16.

Margo Leavin Gallery, Los Angeles. *Cast, Carved, and Constructed,* Aug. 1–Sept. 19.
Muchnic, Suzanne. "A 'Cast' of 21 at Leavin Gallery." *Los Angeles Times* (Los Angeles), Aug. 28, 1981, part 6, p. 2.

The Museum of Modern Art, New York. *Words and Pictures,* Aug. 20–Oct. 6.

Whitney Museum of American Art, Fairfield County, Stamford, Connecticut. *A Tradition Established: 1940–1970, Selections from the Permanent Collection of the Whitney Museum of American Art,* Sept. 4–Oct. 14. Cat., text by Lisa Phillips.

Akron Art Museum, Ohio. *The Image in American Painting and Sculpture 1950–1980,* Sept. 12–Nov. 8.

Pratt Manhattan Center Gallery, New York. *For Love and Money: Dealers Choose,* Sept. 14–Oct. 10. Cat., text by Ellen Schwartz and statements by gallery dealers. Traveled to Hartwick College Museums, Oneonta, New York, Jan. 14–Feb. 15, 1982.

Neuberger Museum, State University of New York, Purchase. *Soundings,* Sept. 20–Dec. 23. Cat., texts by Suzanne Delehanty, Dore Ashton, Germano Celant and Lucy Fischer.
Wooster, Ann-Sargent. "Art Sounds." *Art in America* (New York), vol. 70, no. 2, Feb. 1982, pp. 116–25.

Solomon & Co., New York. *Group Exhibition,* Oct.–Nov.

Städtisches Kunsthalle, Dusseldorf. *Black,* Oct. 16–Dec. 6.

Musej Primenjene Umetnosti, Belgrade, Yugoslavia. *Art of Paper—Art on Paper,* Oct. 29–Nov. 22. Organized by the State University of New York, Albany.

B.R. Kornblatt Gallery, Washington, D.C. *10 Paintings and 2 Sculptures from the 60's,* Nov. 7–Dec. 10.

Castelli Feigen Corcoran, New York. *Group Show,* Nov. 14–Dec. 12.

Haus der Kunst. Munich. *Amerikanische Malerei: 1930–1980,* Nov. 14–Jan. 31, 1982. Cat., texts by Thomas Armstrong and Bernd Growe.
Weskott, Hanne. "Ausstellungen: Deutschland: München: Haus der Kunst, Austellung: Amerikanische Malerei 1930–1980." *Pantheon* (Munich), vol. 150, no. 1, Jan./Feb./Mar. 1982, pp. 60–62.

Edward Thorp Gallery, New York. *Annual Contemporary Drawing Exhibition,* Nov. 14–Dec. 31.

Contemporary Arts Museum, Houston. *Events: Artists in Collaboration,* Dec. 8–Feb. 21, 1982.

1982

Grace Borgenicht Gallery/Terry Dintenfass Gallery, New York. *20 Galleries/20 Years,* Jan 9.–Feb. 4.

Rosa Esman Gallery, New York. *A Curator's Choice: 1942–63 (A Tribute to Dorothy Miller),* Feb. 6–Mar. 6.

The Museum of Modern Art, New York. *A Century of Modern Drawings,* Mar. 1–16.

Marisa del Re Gallery, Inc., New York. *Selected Works on Paper I,* Mar. 2–Apr. 3.

Neuenational Galerie, West Berlin. *Sammlung Dr. Erich Marx: Beuys, Rauschenberg, Twombly, Warhol*, Mar. 10–Apr. 12. Cat., text by Heiner Bastian. Traveled to Städtisches Museum Abteiberg, Monchengladbach, West Germany.
  Onff, H. "Sammlung Dr. Erich Marx: Beuys, Rauschenberg, Twombly, Warhol." *Kunstwerk* (Stuttgart), vol. 35, no. 3, June 1982, pp. 77–78.

Janie C. Lee Gallery, Houston. *Janie C. Lee Honoring Leo Castelli*, Mar. 21–Apr.

Marisa del Re Gallery, Inc., New York. *Selected Works on Paper II*, Apr. 6–29.

Stedelijk Museum, Amsterdam. *'60–'80 attitudes/concepts/images: A Selection from Twenty Years of Visual Arts*, Apr. 9–July 11. Cat., texts by Edy de Wilde, George Weissman, Ad Petersen, Gijs van Tuyl, Wim Beeren, Antje von Graevenitz and Cor Blok.
  MPA. "Exhibition: Amsterdam 60s–80s." *Studio International* (London), vol. 195, no. 996, Sept. 1982, p. 67.

Root Art Center, Hamilton College, Clinton, New York. *Prints and Drawings by Contemporary Masters*, Apr. 15–May 23.

The Museum of Fine Arts, Houston. *Miró in America*, Apr. 21–June 27. Cat., texts by Duncan MacMillan, Judith McCandless and Barbara Rose.

La Jolla Museum of Contemporary Art, California. *Castelli and His Artists: Twenty-five Years*, Apr. 23–June 6. Organized by the Aspen Center for the Visual Arts, Colorado. Cat., texts by Julie Augur, Philip Yenawine and Calvin Tomkins. Traveled to Aspen Center for the Visual Arts, Colorado, June 17–Aug. 7; Leo Castelli Gallery, New York, Sept. 11–Oct. 9; Portland Center for the Visual Arts, Oregon, Oct. 22–Dec. 3; Laguna Gloria Art Museum, Austin, Dec. 17–Feb. 13, 1983.

Whitney Museum of American Art, New York. *Abstract Drawings: 1911–1981*, May 5–July 11.

Larry Gagosian Gallery, Los Angeles. *Works on Paper*, May 22–June 26.

The National Gallery of Art, Washington, D.C. *20th Century Masters: The Thyssen-Bornemisza Collection*, May 30–Sept. 8. Organized and circulated by the International Exhibitions Foundation, Washington, D.C. Cat., text by William S. Lieberman. Traveled to Wadsworth Atheneum, Hartford, Connecticut, Oct. 1–Nov. 28; The Toledo Museum of Art, Ohio, Dec. 17–Feb. 20, 1983; Seattle Art Museum, Mar. 15–May 15, 1983; San Francisco Museum of Modern Art, June 2–July 31, 1983; The Metropolitan Museum of Art, New York, Aug. 30–Nov. 27, 1983; Phoenix Art Museum, Jan. 6–Mar. 2, 1984.
  Wilson, William. "Playing up a Baronial Collection." *Los Angeles Times* (Los Angeles), June 12, 1983, "Calendar" sec., p. 88.

  Miedinski, Charles. "Collecting Powerful Art," *Artweek* (Oakland), July 16, 1983, p. 4.

Leo Castelli Gallery, New York. *New Work by Gallery Artists*, June 1–Sept. 19.

Sonnabend Gallery, New York. *Group Show*, Summer.

Galerie Bischofberger, Zurich. *Homage to Leo Castelli*, June 15–Sept. 4.

The Solomon R. Guggenheim Museum, New York. *The New York School: Four Decades: Guggenheim Collection and Major Loans*, July 1–Aug. 29. Cat., text by Lisa Dennison.
  Russell, John. "Art: Guggenheim Tracks Down New York School." *The New York Times* (New York), July 2, 1982.

  Wolff, Theodore F. "When the New York School Was Tops." *Christian Science Monitor* (Boston), July 12, 1982.

Contemporary Arts Center, Cincinnati. *Drawings from the Collection of Agnes Gund Saalfield*, July 7–Aug. 28.

Contemporary Arts Museum, Houston. *The Americans: The Collage*, July 11–Oct. 3, Cat., text by Linda L. Cathcart.
  Kalil, Susie. "'Americans: The Collage': Review." *The Houston Post* (Houston), July 18, 1982, pp. 1 AA, 16 AA.

  Johnson, Patricia C. "Amusements: Art: American Collages spotlighted in stunning don't-miss CAM exhibit." *The Houston Chronicle* (Houston), July 21, 1982, sec. 6, p. 6.

  Knaff, Deborah L. "Collage captures current whimsy." *The Rice Thresher* (Houston), Aug. 20, 1982, p. 7.

  Kalil, Susie. "American Collage since 1950." *Artweek* (Oakland), vol. 13, no. 30, Sept. 18, 1982, p. 1.

  Rose, Barbara. "Talking about Art: Photos from a cold climate…more artworks by Scandinavians…collages made in U.S.A." *Vogue* (New York), vol. 172, no. 10, Oct. 1982, p. 135.

Avery Center for the Visual Arts, The Bard College Center, Annandale-on-Hudson, New York. *The Rebounding Surface*, Aug. 15–Sept. 24.

Downey Museum of Art, California. *The Written Word*, Sept. 9–Oct. 17.

CDS Gallery, New York. *Renate Ponsold*, Sept. 12–Nov. 15.

Ethniki Pinakothiki and Alexandre Soutzos Museum, Athens, Greece. *American Painting 1900–1982*, Sept. 20–Nov. 7. Cat., texts by Dimitris Papastamos and Barbara Rose.

The Heath Gallery, Inc., Atlanta. *Out of the South: An Exhibition of Artists Born in the South.* Oct. 5–Nov. 11. Cat., text by Donald B. Kuspit.

Sidney Janis Gallery, New York. *The Expressionist Image: American Art from Pollock to Today*, Oct. 9–30.

Daniel Wolf, Inc., New York. *Photographs By/Photographs In*, Oct. 14–Nov. 13.
  Grundberg, Andy. "Photography View: Artist's Works Are at the Center of the Action." *The New York Times* (New York), Oct. 3, 1982, sec. 2, p. 27.

  Smith, Paul. "Photographs By/Photographs In." *Arts* (New York), vol. 57, no. 4, Dec. 1982, p. 9.

Acquavella Galleries, Inc., New York. *XIX & XX Century Drawings, Watercolors, Pastels, Gouaches, Collages*, Oct. 21–Nov. 24. Cat.

Contemporary Arts Museum, Houston. *In Our Time: Houston's Contemporary Arts Museum 1948–1982*, Oct. 23–Jan. 2, 1983. Cat., texts by Linda L. Cathcart, Marti Mayo and Cheryl A. Brutvan.
  Johnson, Patricia C. "The Fascinating history and heritage of the CAM." *The Houston Chronicle* (Houston), Oct. 31, 1982, "Zest" sec., pp. 16, 20.

  Kalil, Susie. "Art: 'In Our Time': Review." *The Houston Post* (Houston), Oct. 31, 1982, pp. 1F, 17F.

  Lunn, Judy. "Exhibits: A forward-looking art museum takes time to look back." *Houston Goodlife Magazine* (Houston), Nov. 1982, p. 10.

  Knaff, Deborah L. "*In Our Time* Celebrates CAM's brief but glorious past." *The Rice Thresher* (Houston), Nov. 5, 1982, p. 15.

Fine Arts Museum of Long Island, Hempstead, New York. *The New Explosion: Paper Art*, Nov. 7–Jan. 13, 1983. Cat., text by Eleanor Blomenhaft. Traveled to CDS Gallery, New York, Feb. 15–Jan. 13, 1983; Byer Museum of the Arts, Evanston, Illinois, Oct. 1–Dec. 31, 1983.
  Harrison, Helen A. "Exploring the Possibilities of Paper." *The New York Times* (New York), Dec. 19, 1982, Long Island sec., p. 28.

Institute of Contemporary Art, Boston. *Art & Dance: Images from the Modern Dialogue 1890–1980*, Nov. 9–Jan. 8, 1983. Cat., texts by Marianne Martin, David Vaughan, Deborah Jowitt and others. Traveled to The Toledo Museum of Art, Ohio, Mar. 6–Apr. 24; The Neuberger Museum, State University of New York, Purchase, June 25–Sept. 25, 1983.
  Acocella, Joan Ross. "The Nation, Purchase, Art + Dance, Neuberger Museum." *Art News* (New York), vol. 82, no. 9, Nov. 1983, pp. 135–36.

Marilyn Pearl Gallery, New York. *Painted Objects*, Dec. 4–Jan. 8, 1983.

Thomas Segal Gallery Alternative Space, Boston. *Big in Boston*, Dec. 10–June 1983.

Betty Parsons Gallery, New York. Dec. 11–22.

Margo Leavin Gallery, Los Angeles. *Group Show*, Dec.

1983
Sunderland Arts Center, England. *Paper as Image*, Jan. 22–Feb. 19. Cat., text by S. Turner. Traveled in Great Britain.

Daniel Weinberg Gallery, Los Angeles. *Drawing Conclusions —A Survey of American Drawings: 1958–1963*, Jan. 29–Feb. 26. Traveled to Daniel Weinberg Gallery, San Francisco, Mar. 9–Apr. 9.

La Jolla Museum of Contemporary Art, California. *A Contemporary Collection on Loan From the Rothschild Bank AG, Zurich*, Feb. 26–Apr. 3. Cat., text by Robert McDonald.

Institute of Contemporary Art, University of Pennsylvania, Philadelphia. *Connections: Bridges/Ladders/Ramps/Staircases/Tunnels*, Mar. 11–Apr. 24. Cat., texts by Janet Kardon and Hal Foster.

Salander-O'Reilly Galleries, New York. *Selections from the Rose Art Museum*, Apr. 6–30.

The Aldrich Museum of Contemporary Art, Ridgefield, Connecticut. *Changes*, May 22–Sept. 11. Cat., texts by Larry Aldrich and Dorothy Mayhall.

Leo Castelli Gallery, New York. *Drawings/Photographs*, Summer.

Leo Castelli Gallery/142 Greene Street, New York. *Sculpture*, Summer.

Sonnabend Gallery, New York, *Group Show*, Summer.

Whitney Museum of American Art, Downtown Branch at Federal Hall, New York. *The Comic Art Show*, July 18–Aug. 26. Cat., texts by John Carlin, Sheena Wagstaff, Richard Marshall, Jerry Robinson, Gary Groth, Kim Thompson and J. Hoberman.

Thomas Babeor Gallery, La Jolla, California. *Summer Selections 1983*, July 22–Sept. 3.

Museo Angel Orensanz y Artes de Serrablo, Sabinanigo, Spain. *Sculpture. Drama. Landscape*, Aug. 13–Sept. 7. Traveled to Leonado Galeria de Arte, Saragoza, Spain, Sept. 13–Oct. 11.

Paula Cooper Gallery, New York, in conjunction with The Next Wave Fall Festival, Brooklyn Academy of Music, New York. *Stage Model for Set and Reset*, Sept. 13–Oct. 1.

Art for a Nuclear Weapons Freeze, Oct.–Dec., traveled in United States.

Seibu Department Stores, Tokyo. *Homage to Leo Castelli*, opened Oct. 7.

Delahunty Gallery, Dallas. *Contemporary Drawing*, Oct. 8–Nov. 9.

J. Irving Feldman Galleries, Sarasota, Florida. *New Acquisitions*, Oct. 9–Nov. 30.

The Museum of Modern Art, New York. *The Modern Drawing: One Hundred Works on Paper in The Museum of Modern Art*, Oct. 26–Jan. 3, 1984. Cat., text by John Elderfield.

Allentown Art Museum, Pennsylvania. *Art of the Comic Strip*, Nov. 6–Feb. 26, 1984.

Harcourts Contemporary, San Francisco. *Made in America*, Nov. 11–Dec. 31.

The New Britain Museum of American Art, Connecticut. *Fragment/Fragmentary/Fragmentation*, Nov. 13–Dec. 31. Cat., texts by Daniel DuBois and Martha Scott.

The Solomon R. Guggenheim Museum, New York. *Trends in Post-War American and European Art*, Nov. 8–27.

Sonnabend Gallery, New York. *Works on Paper: Group Show*, Nov. 19–Dec. 17.

The Museum of Contemporary Art, Los Angeles. *The First Show: Paintings and Sculpture from Eight Collections*, Nov. 23–Feb. 19, 1984. Cat., texts by Julia Brown, Pontus Hulten and Susan C. Larsen.
  Wilson, William. "Temporary Contemporary: Its Time Is Now." *Los Angeles Times* (Los Angeles), Nov. 20, 1983, "Calendar" sec., p. 5.
  Wortz, Melinda. "The First Show at MOCA." *Artweek* (Oakland), vol. 14, no. 43, Dec. 17, 1983, pp. 1, 16.
  Drohojowska, Hunter, "The Nation: Los Angeles: 'The First Show'." *Art News* (New York), vol. 83, no. 3, Mar. 1984, pp. 135–36, 138.

Plagens, Peter. "Exemplary Contemporary." *Art in America* (New York), vol. 72, no. 3, Mar. 1984, pp. 128–37.

The National Museum of Art, Osaka, Japan. *Modern Nude Painting 1880–1980*, closed Dec. 4.

John Michael Kohler Arts Center, Sheboygan, Wisconsin. *The Alternative Image II: Photography on Nonconventional Supports*, Dec. 4–Feb. 12, 1984. Cat., text by Anita Douthat.

Galerie Denise René/Hans Mayer, Dusseldorf. Dec. 15.

Helander/Rubenstein, Palm Beach, Florida. Dec. 1983–Dec. 1984.

Fondation Nationale des Arts Graphiques et Plastiques, Paris.

Frances Godwin & Joseph Ternbach Museum, Queens College, City University of New York, Flushing.

Tokyo Metropolitan Art Museum, Japan. Traveled to The National Museum of Modern Art, Kyoto.

1984

Palm Springs Desert Art Museum, California. *Frederick Weisman Foundation Collection*, Jan. 7–Feb. 26. Cat., text by Frederick S. Wight. (Traveled through 1985.)
  Muchnic, Suzanne. "Palm Springs Flashback to a 'Fun Era'." *Los Angeles Times* (Los Angeles), Feb. 14, 1984, part 6, p. 6.

Center for the Fine Arts, Miami. *In Quest of Excellence: Civic Pride, Patronage, Connoisseurship*, Jan. 14–Apr. 22. Cat., texts by Jan van der Marck, J. Carter Brown, Sherman E. Lee, Agnes Mongan and Philippe de Montebello.

Institute for Art and Urban Resources, P.S. 1, Long Island City, New York. *Salvage: Altered Everyday Objects*, Jan. 22–Mar. 24.

Pratt Manhattan Center Gallery, New York. *From the Beginning*, Feb. 18–Mar. 24.

Helander/Rubenstein, Palm Beach, Florida. Mar.

Janie C. Lee Gallery, Houston. *Master Drawings*, Mar. 17–Apr.
  Johnson, Patricia C. "Drawing Exhibit a Real Joy." *The Houston Chronicle* (Houston), Apr. 8, 1984, "Zest" sec., pp. 36, 37.

Holman Art Gallery, Trenton State College, New Jersey. *Issues (Robert and Nancy Kaye Collection)*, Mar. 28–Apr. 18.

Galerie Biedermann, Munich. *American Drawings*, opened Apr. 12.

Institute for Art and Urban Resources, P.S. 1, Long Island City, New York. *New Portrait*, Apr. 15–June 10.

Hirschl & Adler Modern, New York. *The Skowhegan Celebration Exhibition*, May 2–31. Cat., text by Calvin Tomkins.

Stedelijk Museum, Amsterdam. *Summer Exhibition/20 Years of Collecting*, Summer.

Venice Biennale, Italy. *XII Esposizione Internazionale d'Arte. La Biennale di Venezia*, June. Cat., texts by Paolo Portoghesi, Maurizio Calvesi, Marisa Vescovo, Giuseppe Mazzanol, John Roberts, Flavio Caroli and Franco Farina.

Los Angeles County Museum of Art. *Olympian Gestures*, June 7–Oct. 7.

Art Center College of Design, Pasadena, California. *Castelli at Art Center*, June 25–July 21.

John Michael Kohler Arts Center, Sheboygan, Wisconsin. *Fiber Crosscurrents*, June 24–Aug. 26.

Fuller Goldeen Gallery, San Francisco. *50 Artists/50 States*, July 12–Aug. 25.

Philippe Bonnafont Gallery, San Francisco. *The Artist & The Theater*, July 11–Aug. 11.

Museum of Contemporary Art, Los Angeles. *Automobile and Culture*, July 21–Jan. 6, 1985. Cat., texts by Pontus Hulten, Lord Montagu of Beaulieu, Gerald Silk, Henry Flood Robert, Jr., Strother McMinn and Angelo Tito Anselmi. Traveled to Detroit Institute for the Arts as *Automobile and Culture: Detroit Style*, June 9– Sept. 9, 1985.
    Ianco-Starvels, Josine. "Art News: The Crash of Cars and Culture." *Los Angeles Times* (Los Angeles), July 15, 1984, "Calendar" sec., p. 78.
    Wilson, William. "The Automobile as Artistic Challenge." *Los Angeles Times* (Los Angeles), July 20, 1984, part 6, p. 2.
    Blumfield, John. "'Automobile and Culture,' Museum of Contemporary Art." *Artforum* (New York), vol. 23, no. 3, Nov. 1984, p. 110.

Museum of Fine Arts, Boston. *10 Painters and Sculptors Draw*, Aug. 1–Sept. 30.

Harm Bouckaert Gallery, New York. *Synthetic Art*, Sept. 6–Oct. 6.

Thorpe Intermedia Gallery, Sparkill, New York. *Out of Context*, Sept. 16–Oct. 21. Cat., text by Rosalie Schwartz.

Whitney Museum of American Art, New York. *BLAM! The Explosion of Pop, Minimalism and Performance 1958–1964*, Sept. 19–Dec. 2. Cat., texts by Barbara Haskell and John G. Hanhardt.
    Glueck, Grace. "Art: Exploring 6 Years of Pop and Minimalism." *The New York Times* (New York), Sept. 28, 1984, p. 27C.

The Village Voice (New York), Oct. 16, 1984, p. 109.

Danto, Arthur C. "Art: Blam! The Explosion of Pop, Minimalism and Performance, 1958–1964." *The Nation* (New York), vol. 239, no. 12, Oct. 20, 1984, pp. 390–93.

Larson, Kay. "Art: Pop in Perspective." *New York* (New York), vol. 17, no. 42, Oct. 22, 1984, pp. 140–41.

Kutner, Janet. "On Exhibit: New York galleries, museums show diverse art." *Dallas Morning News* (Dallas), Oct. 25, 1984, pp. 1F, 4F.

Russell, John. "When Art Came Out of the Studio and Mingled." *The New York Times* (New York), Oct. 28, 1984, sec. 2, p. 33.

Tomkins, Calvin. "The Art World: Talismans." *The New Yorker* (New York), Oct. 29, 1984, pp. 120–21.

Wilson, William. "Finally, An Artful Look at the '60s and '70s." *Los Angeles Times* (Los Angeles), Nov. 4, 1984, "Calendar" sec., p. 82.

Visual Arts Museum, School of Visual Arts, New York. *Collage Expanded*, Oct. 1–20. Cat., text by Jeanne Siegel.
    Lichtenstein, Therese. "Arts reviews: Collage Expanded." *Arts* (New York), vol. 59, no. 4, Dec. 1984, pp. 34–35.

Blum Helman, New York. *Drawings*, Oct. 10–Nov. 3.

Castelli Graphics, New York. *New Drawings by Castelli Artists*, Oct. 13–Nov. 3.

Marisa del Re Gallery, Inc., New York. *Masters of the Sixties: From New Realism to Pop Art*, Nov. 7–Dec. 1, 1984. Cat., text by Sam Hunter.
    Raynor, Vivien. "Art: Bronzes and Drawings by Saint Gaudens; Masters of the Sixties." *The New York Times* (New York), Nov. 30, 1984, sec. 3, p. 26.
    Heartney, Eleanor. "Masters of the Sixties." *Art News* (New York), vol. 84, no. 2, Feb. 1985, p. 136.
    Kuspit, Donald. "'Masters of the Sixties: From New Realism to Pop Art,' Marisa del Re Gallery." *Artforum* (New York), vol. 23, no. 7, Mar. 1985, p. 98.

Sonnabend Gallery, New York. *Group Show*, Nov. 24– Dec. 15

Blum Helman, New York. *Enzo Cucchi, Robert Rauschenberg, Donald Sultan: New Paintings*, Dec. 5– Jan. 1985.

Rosa Esman Gallery, New York. *Drawings from Kliun to Kiefer*, Dec. 8–Jan. 5, 1985.

1985

Marisa del Re Gallery, Inc., New York. *Recent Acquisitions*, Jan. 9–Feb. 2.

The Art Museum, Princeton University, New Jersey. *Selections from the Ileana and Michael Sonnabend Collection: Works from the 1950s and 1960s*, Feb. 3–June 9. Traveled to the Archer M. Huntington Art Gallery, The University of Texas at Austin, Sept. 8–Oct. 27; Walker Art Center, Minneapolis, Nov. 23–Mar. 9, 1986. Cat., texts by Sam Hunter and Robert Pincus-Witten.

The Museum of Contemporary Art, Los Angeles. *The Museum of Contemporary Art: The Panza Collection*, Feb. 9–Sept. 29. Cat., texts by Richard Koshalek and Kerry Brougher.
> Muchnic, Suzanne. "Art Review: A Stunning Aesthetic Event." *Los Angeles Times* (Los Angeles), Feb. 11, 1985, sec. 4, pp. 1,3.

Art Gallery of New South Wales, Sydney, Australia. *Pop Art: 1955–1970*, Feb. 26–Apr. 14. Organized under the auspices of the International Council of The Museum of Modern Art, New York. Cat., text by Henry Geldzahler. Traveled in Australia to Queensland Art Gallery, Brisbane, May 1–June 6; National Gallery of Victoria, Melbourne, June 26–Aug. 11.

Rice Museum, Institute for the Arts, Rice University, Houston. *Twenty-seven Ways of Looking at American Drawing 1930–1980*, Feb. 26–Apr. 7. Expanded version traveled to Ecole Nationale Supérieure des Beaux-Arts, Chapelle des Petits Augustins, Paris, as *Cinquante Ans de Dessins Américains 1930–1980*, May 3–July 13.
> Johnson, Patricia C. "Art: 'Drawing' Comparisons." *The Houston Chronicle* (Houston), Mar. 10, 1985, "Zest" sec., p. 36.

Kunsthalle Tubingen, West Germany. *7000 Eichen*, Mar. 2–Apr. 14. Cat., text by Heiner Bastian. Traveled to Kunsthalle Bielefeld, West Germany, June 2–Aug 11; Staatliche und Städtische Kunstsammlungen Kassel, Aug. 25–Sept. 22.

Dracos Art Center, Athens, Greece. *Group Exhibition*, Mar. 4–Apr. 18.

Edith C. Blum Art Institute, The Bard College Center, Annandale-on-Hudson, New York. *The Maximal Implications of the Minimal Line*, Mar. 24–Apr. 28.

Janie C. Lee Gallery, Houston. *Modern American Masters*, Apr. 10–May.
> Johnson, Patricia C. "These Masters Deserve Title." *The Houston Chronicle* (Houston), Apr. 28, 1985, "Zest" sec., p. 16.

The Museum of Modern Art, New York. *Philip Johnson: Selected Gifts*, Apr. 10–Oct. 27.
> Russell, John. "Art: Works Given by Philip Johnson." *The New York Times* (New York), May 11, 1985, p. 17.

Larry Gagosian Gallery, Los Angeles. *60's Color*, Apr. 16–May 11.

The Mayor Gallery, London. *A Tribute to Leo Castelli*, Apr. 16–May 17. Cat., text by Calvin Tomkins.
> Berman, Arthur. "Tribute to Pop Art." *TNT (The News & Travel International)* (London), issue 87, Apr. 30, 1985.

Smith College Museum of Art, Northampton, Massachusetts. *Dorothy C. Miller: With an Eye to American Art*, Apr. 19–June 16.

Nelson-Atkins Museum of Art, Kansas City, Missouri. *The Kansas City Art Institute's First Century*, Apr. 20–May 26.

Acquavella Galleries, Inc., New York. *XIX and XX Century Master Drawings and Watercolors*, Apr. 22–May 24. Cat.

The Aldrich Museum of Contemporary Art, Ridgefield, Connecticut. *The Classic Tradition in Recent Painting and Sculpture*, May 19–Sept. 1. Cat., texts by Larry Aldrich and Dr. Robert P. Metzger.
> Raynor, Vivien. "A Return to Classicism in Ridgefield." *The New York Times* (New York), July 14, 1985, Connecticut sec., p. 24.

City Gallery, City of New York Department of Cultural Affairs, New York. *Paper: From Surface to Form*, June 10–July 6.

The Solomon R. Guggenheim Museum, New York. *Painterly Visions, 1940–1984: The Guggenheim Collection and Major Loans*, June 28–Sept. 3. Brochure, text by Susan Hirschfeld.

The Aldrich Museum of Contemporary Art, Ridgefield, Connecticut. *A Second Talent…*, Sept. 22–Dec. 29.

Selected Bibliography

Bibliography listings are arranged chronologically and consist primarily of articles from 1976 to the present. Selected articles and reviews relating to the "Cardboard" and "Hoarfrost" series, written prior to 1976, are included as well.

Books

Diamondstein, Barbaralee. *Inside New York's Art World.* New York: Rizzoli, 1979.

Tomkins, Calvin. *Off the Wall: Robert Rauschenberg and the Art World of our Time.* Garden City, New York: Doubleday & Company, Inc., 1980.

Rosenthal, Nan. *Robert Rauschenberg.* New York: Abbeville Press, to be published in 1986.

Articles

Shirey, David L. "Rauschenberg Turning to Cardboards." *The New York Times* (New York), Oct. 23, 1971, p. 23.

Schjeldahl, Peter. "Rauschenberg Just Won't Be Boxed In." *The New York Times* (New York), Oct. 31, 1971, sec. 2, p. 21.

S[iegel], J[eanne]. "Reviews and Previews: Robert Rauschenberg's Cardboards…" *Art News* (New York), vol. 70, no. 8, Dec. 1971, p. 19.

Domingo, Willis. "In the Galleries: Robert Rauschenberg …Castelli." *Arts Magazine* (New York), vol. 46, no. 3, Dec. 1971–Jan. 1972, p. 60.

Pincus-Witten, Robert. "Rauschenberg: Cardbirds and Cardboards." *Artforum* (New York), vol. 10, no. 5, Jan. 1972, pp. 79–80.

Henry, Gerrit. "Personal Retrenchment: Gerrit Henry Considers the Recent Work of Robert Rauschenberg." *Art and Artists* (London), vol. 6, no. 11, Feb. 1972, pp. 42–45.

Dreiss, Joseph. "Robert Rauschenberg, Leo Castelli (Uptown & Downtown), Sonnabend." *Arts Magazine* (New York), vol. 49, no. 6, Feb. 1975, p. 16.

Bourdon, David. "Rauschenberg's Hoarfrost Causes Shivers of Delight." *The Village Voice* (New York), Mar. 10, 1975, p. 84.

Smith, Roberta. "Reviews: Robert Rauschenberg, Castelli Gallery downtown and Sonnabend." *Artforum* (New York), vol. 13, no. 7, Mar. 1975, p. 66.

Forsyth, S. "Silks and Satins." *Arts Review* (London), vol. 27, no. 8, Apr. 18, 1975, p. 227.

Larson, Philip. "Robert Rauschenberg." *Arts Magazine* (New York), vol. 49, no. 8, Apr. 1975, p. 78.

Abadie, Daniel. "Les Images gelées de Robert Rauschenberg." *Art Press* (Paris), no. 19, July–Aug. 1975, pp. 16–17.

Chieco, Giuseppe with Robert Rauschenberg. "Dai Combine Paintings ai Jammers. Intervista con Robert Rauschenberg a cura di Giuseppe Chieco." *Le Arti* (Milan), vol. 26, no. 3, Mar. 1976, pp. 47–50.

Glueck, Grace. "Art People: New Chief in the Bronx, A Philadelphia Giant and Dr. Perry's Firsts." *The New York Times* (New York), July 2, 1976, sec. 3, p. 21.

Iden, Peter. "Ich bemuhe mich, mit dem, was ich tue, nicht vertraut zu sein." *Kunstwerk* (Stuttgart), vol. 29, no. 6, Nov. 1976, pp. 6–7.

Hughes, Robert. "The Most Living Artist." *Time* (New York), vol. 108, no. 22, Nov. 29, 1976, pp. 54–62.

Rose, Barbara. "Rauschenberg: The Artist as Witness." *Vogue* (New York), vol. 167, no. 2, Feb. 1977, pp. 174–75, 220, 226.

Glueck, Grace. "Art People." *The New York Times* (New York), Mar. 11, 1977, sec. 3, p. 22.

Glueck, Grace. "Art People." *The New York Times* (New York), Mar. 25, 1977, sec. 3, p. 19.

Smith, Philip. "To and about Robert Rauschenberg." *Arts Magazine* (New York), vol. 51, no. 7, Mar. 1977, pp. 120–21.

Tomkins, Calvin. "Robert Rauschenberg." *Parachute* (Montreal), no. 6, Spring 1977, pp. 22–24.

Brunnell, L. "Cunningham et Cage: pour les oiseaux— MC = E². " *Art Press* (Paris), no. 6, Apr. 1977, pp. 26–27.

Rosenberg, Harold. "Souvenirs of an Avant-Garde." *The New Yorker* (New York), vol. 53, no. 13, May 16, 1977, pp. 123–28.

Roth, Moira. "The Aesthetic of Indifference." *Artforum* (New York), vol. 16, no. 3, Nov. 1977, pp. 46–53.

Bernstein, Roberta. "Robert Rauschenberg's 'Rebus'." *Arts Magazine* (New York), vol. 52, no. 5, Jan. 1978, pp. 138–41.

"The 'Vasari' Diary: More Dangerous than Generals." *Art News* (New York), vol. 77, no. 2, Feb. 1978, pp. 22–24.

Kasher, Steven. "The Substance of Paper." *Artforum* (New York), vol. 16, no. 7, Mar. 1978, pp. 26–28.

Greenberg, Clement. "L'avanguardia: quando smette di essere avanguardia?" *Bolaffiarte* (Milan), no. 81, vol. 9, Summer 1978, pp. 9–10.

Hopkins, T. "Revolutionary for the hell of it." *MacLean's* (Toronto), vol. 91, Oct. 2, 1978, pp. 70–71.

Perry, Arthur. "A Conversation between Robert Rauschenberg and Arthur Perry." *Artmagazine* (Toronto), vol. 10, no. 41, Nov.–Dec. 1978, pp. 31–35.

Bongard, W. "Non è vero che i quadri siano cari: quasi sempre sono sottocosto. Quanto costa diventare Rauschenberg?" *Bolaffiarte* (Milan), no. 88, vol. 10, Apr.–May 1979, pp. 54–55.

Goldstein, Carl. "Teaching Modernism: What Albers learned in The Bauhaus and taught to Rauschenberg, Noland and Hesse." *Arts Magazine* (New York), vol. 54, no. 4, Dec. 1979, pp. 108–16.

Scarpetta, G. "Trisha Brown: le mouvement brownien." *Art Press* (Paris), no. 33, Nov. 1979, p. 8.

Burstein, Patricia. "In His Art and Life, Robert Rauschenberg is a Man who Steers His Own Daring Course." *People* (New York), vol. 13, no. 20, May 19, 1980, pp. 99–104.

Deitz, Paula. "The Combine Painter." *The New York Times* (New York), May 25, 1980, sec. 7, pp. 9, 18.

Broyard, Anatole. "Books of the Times: A Question of Etiquette." *The New York Times* (New York), May 31, 1980, p. 21.

Crimp, Douglas. "On the Museum's Ruins." *October* (Cambridge, Mass.), no. 13, Summer 1980, pp. 41–58.

Owens, Craig. "The Allegorical Impulse: Towards a Theory of Postmodernism (Part 2)." *October* (Cambridge, Mass.), no. 13, Summer 1980, pp. 59–80.

Forsling, Stephen. "Fizzles, Savage Breeze, Kitty Hawk and a Message from Degas." *Art News* (New York), vol. 79, no. 7, Sept. 1980, pp. 127–28.

Gruen, J. "Robert Rauschenberg: et Publikum pa en" *Louisiana Revy* (Humlebaek), vol. 21, no. 1, Sept. 1980, pp. 34–42.

Parinaud, André. "Robert Rauschenberg interviewet af Andre Parinaud." *Louisiana Revy* (Humlebaek), vol. 21, no. 1, Sept. 1980, pp. 16–18.

Wivel, M. "Get up, get out, get into something new." *Louisiana Revy* (Humlebaek), vol. 21, no. 1, Sept. 1980, pp. 18–29.

Morris, Gay. "When Artists Use Photographs: Is it Fair Use, Legitimate Transformation or Rip-off?" *Art News* (New York), vol. 80, no. 1, Jan. 1981, pp. 102–106.

Ratcliff, Carter. "Mostly Monochrome." *Art in America* (New York), vol. 69, no. 4, Apr. 1981, pp. 111-31.

Cranshaw, R. and Lewis, A. "Re-reading Rauschenberg." *Artscribe* (London), no. 29, June 1981, pp. 44–51.

Grundberg, Andy. "Another Side of Rauschenberg." *The New York Times* (New York), Oct. 18, 1981, sec. 6, pp. 43–46, 113, 116.

Gottleib, C. "Self-portraiture in Postmodern Art." *Wallraf-Richartz Jahrbuch* (Cologne), vol. 42, 1981, pp. 284–86.

Bendiner, Kenneth. "Robert Rauschenberg's 'Canyon'." *Arts Magazine* (New York), vol. 56, no. 10, June 1982, pp. 57–59.

Rohter, Larry. "China: A Brush with the Master." *Newsweek* (New York), vol. 100, no. 5, Aug. 2, 1982, p. 40.

Secrest, Meryle. "Leo Castelli: Dealing In Myths." *Art News* (New York), vol. 81, no. 6, Summer 1982, pp. 66–72.

Buchloh, Benjamin H. D. "Allegorical Procedures: Appropriation and Montage in Contemporary Art." *Artforum* (New York), vol. 21, no. 1, Sept. 1982, pp. 43–56.

Gardner, Paul. "Will Success Spoil Bob & Jim, Louise & Larry?" *Art News* (New York), vol. 81, no. 9, Nov. 1982, pp. 102–109.

Millet, C. and Solomon, M. "Robert Rauschenberg à travers le monde." *Art Press* (Paris), no. 65, Dec. 1982, pp. 4–7.

Rowes, Barbara. "Painter Robert Rauschenberg Takes a Trip to China and Pops Back with New Shows and New Vitality." *People* (New York), vol. 19, no. 3, Jan. 24, 1983, pp. 82–83.

Steinbrink, Mark. "Why Artists Design for Paul Taylor." *The New York Times* (New York), Apr. 3, 1983, sec. 2, pp. 1, 24.

"Interior Design Market: Japanese Ceramic Murals by Robert Rauschenberg." *Interior Design* (New York), vol. 54, no. 5, May 1983, p. 172.

"Robert Rauschenberg Ceramics." *Ceramics Monthly* (Columbus), vol. 31, no. 5, May 1983, pp. 39–41.

Rosenthal, Mark. "The Structured Subject in Contemporary Art: Reflections on Work in the Twentieth-Century Galleries." *Philadelphia Museum of Art Bulletin* (Philadelphia), vol. 79, no. 340, Fall 1983, pp. 1–24.

Cabutti, L. "Il rinascimento di Rauschenberg." *Arte* (Milan), no. 133, vol. 13, Sept. 1983, pp. 62–67.

Kisselgoff, Anna. "Dance: Premiere of 'Set and Reset'." *The New York Times* (New York), Oct. 23, 1983, p. 62.

Brenson, Michael. "Art People: Rauschenberg's Giant Photo." *The New York Times* (New York), Oct. 29, 1983, sec. 3, p. 21.

Russell, John. "Today's Artists Are in Love with the Stage." *The New York Times* (New York), Oct. 30, 1983, sec. 2, pp. 1, 26.

McEvilley, Thomas. "Freeing Dance from the Web." *Artforum* (New York), vol. 22, no. 5, Jan. 1984, pp. 54–57.

"All Aboard the Shuttle." *Life* (New York), vol. 7, no. 11, Oct. 1984, pp. 64–78.

Hunter, Fredericka. "Rauschenberg." *Ultra* (Houston), vol. 4, no. 4, Dec. 1984, pp. 124–27, 190–91.

Krasnow, Iris. "Art: Rauschenberg: After all these years, this native Texan is still the bad boy of the art world." *The Houston Post* (Houston), Dec. 16, 1984, p. 9F.

Photograph credits

Rick Begneaud, frontispiece
Terry Van Brunt, pp. 15, 18, 27
George Lange Photography, p. 17
eeva-inkeri, p. 14
Lois Greenfield, p. 20
Rick Gardner, p. 21
Theo Westenberger, p. 22
Michael Abramson, p. 22
Eric Pollitzer, p. 27
Glenn Steigelman Inc., pp. 28, 29, 31, 32, 38, 39, 40, 45, 46, 47, 48, 49, 53, 54, 56, 58, 59, 60, 61, 62, 64, 65
Emil Fray, pp. 30, 51, 57, 63
Alex Mirzaoff, pp. 33, 34, 35, 36, 37
Zindman/Fremont, pp. 41, 42, 43, 44, 50, 52, 55

Designed by **Creel Morrell Inc**
Typesetting by **Professional Typographers,** Houston
5000 copies printed by **Wetmore & Co.**
Distributed nationally by **Texas Monthly Press**
P.O. Box 1569, Austin, Texas 78767-1569

Cover:

**The Vain Convoy of Europe Out West
(Kabal American Zephyr)** 1982
Solvent transfer, acrylic and collage on wood veneer with objects
74 x 96½ x 41½"
Courtesy of the artist